# Own YOUR WORTH

---

*Discovering the Truth in the Midst of Lies*

**JESSICA VAUGHN**

© 2018 Jessica Vaughn. All rights reserved, including the right to reproduce this book or portions of this book in any form whatsoever without the prior written permission of the copyright holder.

Editor: Jodi Brandon
Designer: Jess Creatives

Disclaimer
The information provided within is for general informational purposes only. The author has made every effort to include information up-to-date and correct, but there are no representations or warranties, express or implied, about the completeness, accuracy, reliability, suitability or availability with respect to the information, products, services, or related graphics contained within. Any use of this information is at your own risk.

*Dedication*

To the woman who feels left out, unseen, lost, broken, or confused.
God sees you.

To Jon. You make my life better, never boring, and always beautiful!

## Table of Contents

Opening Thoughts: The Beginning of a Season............7

Chapter 1: Failing Successfully........................................13

Chapter 2: The Stealer of My Peace ...............................31

Chapter 3: Returning Home ............................................51

Chapter 4: Mediocre ........................................................69

Chapter 5: For the Love of Money.................................83

Chapter 6: New Wineskin................................................99

Chapter 7: The Heart of the Father................................115

Closing Thoughts: The End of a Season .........................129

About the Author.............................................................133

## *Opening Thoughts:*
# The Beginning of a Season

≡

Welcome to season three of discovering your worth. If you are wondering what season one and season two had to deal with, then let me give you a quick run-down.

Season one was titled *Know Your Worth*. This season was about how I lost myself in my body image, how my past wouldn't stay out of my present, how and when I discovered my faith, how I got dumped for being too short, and how I met my husband on eHarmony. One thing was true: I put my worth in everything else but Jesus and who He was.

Season two was titled *A Worthy Wife*. This season was all about learning how to date, to be happy single, to understand what it looks like to have a Godly relationship, to communicate and understand your husband, and, most importantly, to be the woman of God He has called you to be in the waiting and when you are married.

Now, enter season three, titled *Own Your Worth*. In this season, I have found that I can know Whose I am, but it doesn't change the fact that I am still human and that "Satan likes to disguise himself as an angel of light" (2 Corinthians 11:14). The first few words or phrases that come to my mind when I think of Satan disguising himself as an angel of like are: *instant results, short-term pleasure, instant gratification, quick fix, lose this fast, have quick reward,* and *overnight success.* All those words appeal to my flesh. My flesh rises and says, "Yes, give me all of that." More. More. More.

I am mistaken for what appears to be good, only to be fooled, misled, and let down. Have you ever been there? Everything quick, instant, and fast can lead us astray and usually offers short-term results. They provide "in the moment enjoyment"—you know, the desires of the flesh that seem so good in the moment but fill you with regret later.

You step out in faith. You think you heard Him right. Only then you begin to question whether you heard Him at all. There are things you will experience that you will never understand nor comprehend with your human mind. The more and more searching you do to try to find the answer to your flesh desires, the more and more lost you begin to feel. Stormie Ormartian wrote in her book *30 Days to Becoming a Woman of Prayer*, "Trust that God has the answer to every question you have, so you stop obsessing over your questions and start trusting His answers."

Season three is going to be about chasing the long-term reward. The real reward. The only reward that our hearts should want. The reward that lasts, that has endless grace and mercy, that forgives when we don't deserve it, that sees our flaws and calls us flawless. Then when we see Jesus face-to-face He will not hesitate to say, "Well done, my good and faithful servant" (Matthew 25:21).

Season three is also going to be about the truth of the "human condition," as Judah Smith likes to say in his sermons. The truth that following Jesus and laying down your life for Him don't come without sacrifice, sometimes feeling alone, and loss. That is the truth. Ministry is messy. Life is messy, and you have an enemy trying to do anything he can to "steal, kill, and destroy" (John 10:10) any area of your life that you allow him to. John 10:10 refers to the enemy as a thief. When we drop our guard, lose our focus, and follow our flesh things get taken and stolen from us. You may not even realize what has been stolen until one day you look for it and realize it is missing.

Author and pastor Dave Early wrote in his books, "Ministry is getting dirty to make others clean." I'm going to talk about the dirty part. The things that few talk about. The things that don't exactly make a ton of people want to follow because it's not instant, quick or fast. More than you would like to admit, you are led by your flesh and you are led by what others are doing around you. It's sometimes just easier to follow the leader and to blend in with the crowd, just in case you realize you were born to stand out and wouldn't want anyone to not like you. (Did that ruffle any feathers? Okay. Good. You were born to stand out. Stop trying to blend in.)

After my first book, *Know Your Worth*, was released I realized a piece of the puzzle that was missing. I can tell you all day who Jesus is, and you can read His word every day, but it's applying His word daily and renewing ourselves to believe and live out the truth that I was missing. What does living out the words *know your worth* mean and look like? It's amazing for us to know who He is, but to believe what He says and live that out is a whole other area that I am going to dive into with this book, season three, *Own Your Worth*.

I'm not sure what made you buy this book. Maybe the title caught your eye. Maybe it was the fact that you are just so tired of living the life you are living and are ready to be set free. To be honest, it doesn't matter why you bought it. It matters that you are here and love yourself enough to stay here to know you are worth more.

You are ready to read this book if you want to go to another level with Him. I am going to ask tough questions—questions that I have had to ask myself many times before in this season of my life. I'll be sharing stories I have yet to talk about anywhere else but here. You get the front-row seat to a season that has challenged me and changed me. A season in which I questioned a lot and doubted a lot, and, let's just say, wasn't always the best example of His word (especially to my husband, Jon). This is real life. I'm human. I'm full of mistakes. You and I are on this journey together. I'm walking with you.

One more thing: Don't worry if you have not read *Know Your*

*Worth* or *A Worthy Wife*. There is time to catch up on them later. You are not behind on my crazy adventures with Jesus. You are right on time with where you need to be now. Each season (or book) has its own experiences, and each season of my life has had its fair share of trials, losses, wins, and gains, pains, and uncertainties.

My biggest prayers for you are that you realize you are not alone, that you can truly conquer anything with Jesus by your side, that you are not defined by the choices you make, and that you know there is always hope for you and it's never too late. Ever. There is no clock or time line in heaven. God's not tapping His toes watching the minutes pass on a timer hoping you get to Him before time runs out. He's there. He's there now with you. Close your eyes right now and let Him in. Let Him hug you, love you, and cuddle you up. Let's quit believing the lies that say it is too late and begin to lift our heads up to a God that says, "You are enough."

*Chapter 1*
# Failing Successfully

≡

I was 20 when I started to gain passion for the fitness world. It was something that I felt like I could control. I could control how much weight I lifted. I could control what I did on a cardio machine. For the first time in my life, I felt like I was finally in control of something. Working out was something that didn't control me or tell me what to do or beat me around. I told my body what to do and what to lift. I always wanted more. I looked forward to going to the gym to see what my body could do. Things took off from there.

The first time I went to college, right out of high school, my major was going to be nutrition. I thought, *This is it. This is what I am meant to do.* After going to college for two years and studying nutrition, I realized how much I didn't enjoy it. It didn't excite me, and I never looked forward to going to class. So, I dropped out. I thought maybe I would take a break. I told myself it would be temporary but also thought maybe college just wasn't for me.

My passion for the fitness world was only gaining momentum at that point. The nutrition aspect wasn't my thing, but I did love how the body could move.

Fast-forward to age 22. I started my own fitness business from home, coaching others online. I finally felt like I had a purpose. Again, I thought to myself, *This is it. This is what I am supposed to be doing.* Quickly after I started my online business, I started training people in person. I became a personal trainer because I wanted people to feel what I felt when I went to the gym. I didn't want them to fear the gym. I wanted them to have confidence in what they could do—in what their body could do.

I was two years older since dropping out of college the first time and starting my own business, and I thought for sure I was more mature and ready to try the college thing again.

I applied for my student loans. I scheduled my classes and changed my major to exercise science. I told myself that this was it, and that I was finally going to get a degree and really work with people. Exercise science to me was more hands-on, more movement, than nutrition. So that had to be it for me, right?

Wrong.

More than a year went by. My online business grew. I started training more clients in person. I became a fitness instructor teaching classes. Yet again, every time I would go to my classes to bring me one step closer to my degree, I hated it. I questioned it so much: *Does it mean I am stupid if I don't have a degree? Maybe some people aren't meant for college? Maybe that just isn't their path? Will people take me seriously if I don't have a degree? Will they want to work with? Am I failure? Will people say to me, "I told you so"?*

The Lord knew how desperately I wanted that degree. I wanted to have that title, the piece of paper that said, "You did it. You have worth. Now go live your life." I knew that it would prove to people I had meaning. It would prove to people that I was smart. I could finally say I was someone.

At the end of the second year, before starting a new semester, I dropped out. My second time dropping out of college. I really thought being more mature and having a different mindset would make going back better, but it didn't. Now I had college debt. I felt like I failed and had no college degree. I thought, *Way to go, Jess!*

I stopped throwing a pity party and said to myself, *No degree. No problem. I'll go get certification on being a personal trainer. I'll learn as much as I can about teaching group fitness classes. I'll invest in as many courses as I can online to grow my business.* More certifications would equal that I was worth more. More people I trained meant I was significant to others.

At about the time I dropped out of college for the second time and focused on my online business, I finally quit my full-time job to pursue all things fitness. I know what you are probably thinking: How did you know when to do it? For me, it was when my income in fitness matched my income at my full-time job. I had to be smart about my decisions because I had a house, bills, and debt. I worked many part-time jobs along with my fitness jobs and full-time job to comfortably leave. It wasn't an easy road for me, and to be honest leaving my full-time job was one of the scariest things ever. My full-time job felt safe—versus being an entrepreneur, which can make you feel not safe at any given moment.

There I was, finally feeling like I was someone again after dropping out of college. I had group fitness certifications. I was teaching at my local college and a few other places. At the time, I was still personal training and helping people get results but without a certification. The local college where I was teaching always had postings about the certifications coming up. This was it: my time to finally feel complete. *I'll get this certification to show people that I did it—that I have arrived at my final destination.*

I signed up for the certification. Got the books. (Have I mentioned yet how much I hate studying?) I put off studying as much as I could. I felt so confident going into that weekend. (This was a certification for which you studied the book together, in person, for two days, then on the second day took the written exam.) I felt prepared because I had worked with so many people. I had learned a lot when I was in college. *I can do this.*

Pencils were ready. It was time for the written exam. (Have I mentioned yet that I'm a terrible test-taker?) I felt confident because I thought I knew what I needed to know. I proceeded to open the test and see long, descriptive paragraphs that reminded me of story problems back when I was in high school. *Oh no! Can I really do this?*

As people started to finish their tests and get up, I became even more nervous and anxious. *Am I not smart enough? Why can't I finish quicker, too?* More people were getting up and I had to keep telling myself to focus. I got so distracted by people getting up and the feelings of me not being smart enough that time was wasted. I forgot to mention that this was a timed test. Take my not-so-good test-taking skills and add in a timer, and that can equal a not-so-good result.

I finished, and I felt good when all was said and done. Then I just had to wait for the results.

During the waiting period, I kept convincing myself that the results didn't matter. I would still go on to do what I felt called to do. After a few weeks went by, one day I arrived to teach class at the college where I taught and was handed my results. I can remember where I was when I read the results: walking down stairs at a pretty slow pace. (Not recommended.) There it was—what I had been waiting for to tell me I was good. To tell me I had meaning.

## The Results Are In

My heart sank. I failed the test by two points.

This was one of those situations when you wish you would have failed by more than two points. I felt like I was so close to meaning something, only to miss it by a couple points. I felt like the biggest failure. I was already training people and helping them, and they loved it, but now without this piece of paper saying I was smart enough to do it, what would I say to them? Did I even want to tell them about my failure? I only told maybe one or two people at the time. I was too ashamed to admit my failure. I was too afraid that people would look at me differently. It was like a deep, dark secret that no one knew and I didn't talk about. I still haven't talked about it much at all until now. Looking back, maybe this was God's way of showing me that I didn't need some test to tell me I was good enough, I was smart enough, or my life had purpose and meaning. (I love His sense of humor and love.)

A test may be no big deal to you. You could be thinking, *Why not just take the test again?* That wasn't an option for me. You must understand how much I wanted meaning and worth in that season of my life. I was turning left and right trying to find it. So, failing that test set me back further into the hole of feeling mediocre. Surely there is something in your life that you have felt shame about, or that made you feel like you will never be successful or amount to anything. It may not be a test like mine, but it's something that meant something to you in that season. Maybe you are in that season now.

Here is what I must say to you—and to me—about all these feelings that keep coming up about being unqualified and not good enough: Jesus died on the cross and when He rose, we rose with Him. That means, I don't qualify myself, other people don't qualify me, and I'm not worthy because someone says I am or by passing a test to tell me I am smart. I am not what I have done, I am who I am because of what He has done.

I know what you are carrying, my friend. You are walking around with shame in your body, brokenness in your heart, and thoughts of how much of a failure you are in your head. Your whole body is consumed with everything the enemy wants you to focus on. We become out of step with the spirit and in step with our flesh.

Galatians 5:17–21 reminds us of this truth:

*The sinful nature wants to do evil, which is just the opposite of what the Spirit wants. And the Spirit gives us desires that are the opposite of what the sinful nature desires. These two forces are constantly fighting each other, so you are not free to carry out your good intentions. But when you are directed by the Spirit, you are not under obligation to the law of Moses.*

*When you follow the desires of your sinful nature, the results are very clear: sexual immorality, impurity, lustful pleasures, idolatry, sorcery, hostility, quarreling, jealousy, outbursts of anger, selfish ambition, dissension, division, envy, drunkenness, wild parties, and other sins like these. Let me tell you again, as I have before, that anyone living that sort of life will not inherit the Kingdom of God.*

Being a college dropout and failing a test don't define who

I am. Nor do I need to carry around any weight (feelings and emotions) with those things. They are facts in my life—things that have indeed happened—but they are not what I choose to define my life by.

Here is your sign. Here is your wake-up call to stop carrying this weight. You are suffocating yourself with this weight. You have exhausted yourself blaming everyone else. You are worn out trying to figure it out. You are tired of feeling this way. Stop. Go to Him. Cry to Him. Repent of your sins. Ask for forgiveness for the things you keep trying to control in your own strength. You are choosing today, right now, to no longer be a victim of your circumstance(s) or what has happened to you or what you have done. Enough is enough. Today, right now, you are declaring and giving it over to Him. He wants you to give it over to Him. He loves you. He is a good Father. It's time to let go of the weight so you can rise.

## Letting Go So You Can Live

When I think about failing successfully, I think about Peter as Jesus was on His way to the cross. Jesus knew Peter was going to deny Him. *"Truly I tell you," Jesus answered, "this very night, before the rooster crows, you will disown me three times"* (Matthew 26:34). This scripture, without a doubt, tells us that Jesus knows us way better than we know ourselves. It also reminds us that He knows our future. Peter's response to Jesus was: *"Even if I have to die with you, I will never disown you." And all the other disciples said the same* (Matthew 26:35).

The course of our life is dictated by the choices and decisions we make every day. There will be choices when you felt like you heard Him right, only to discover that the choice was more about you than Him. You might make a decision that sets you back, even though at the time it seemed like a good idea.

Even though you may make a decision that takes you off His path, He is always looking and ready for you to come back to Him. The choice or decision doesn't have to be the death of your calling. It doesn't have to be the death of you. You are never too far gone. I could have walked away from personal training and teaching fitness classes after failing that test and being a college dropout. Easily. But I didn't. You are not going to give up, either, because of decisions or choices made.

Let's continue this journey with Peter.

He tells Jesus he will die with Him, but then when everything hits the fan and Judas betrays Jesus, Peter is forced to decide quickly whether he will claim to know who Jesus is at all. What was his decision? Matthew 26:69–75 tells us:

*Meanwhile, Peter was sitting outside in the courtyard. A servant girl came over and said to him, "You were one of those with Jesus the Galilean." But Peter denied it in front of everyone. "I don't know what you're talking about," he said. Later, out by the gate, another servant girl noticed him and said to those standing around, "This man was with Jesus of Nazareth." Again, Peter denied it, this time with an oath. "I don't even know the man," he said. A little later some of the other bystanders came over to Peter and said, "You must be one of them; we can tell by your Galilean accent." Peter swore, "A curse on me if I'm lying—I don't know the man!" And immediately the rooster crowed. Suddenly, Jesus' words flashed through Peter's mind: "Before the rooster crows, you will deny three times that you even know me." And he went away, weeping bitterly.*

Can you imagine what Peter was going through emotionally after everything was said and done? Knowing everything Jesus did for him, and how He loved him and told Him that he would die with Him if it came to that, only for Peter to deny Him three times? Scripture tells us that "*he went away, weeping bitterly*" (Matthew 26:75). The definition of those two words gives us an even better example of the emotions Peter was feeling: *Weeping* means "shedding tears." *Bitterly* means "in an angry or hurt way." I am sure Peter was extremely angry at himself and so hurt, too, to know that he betrayed the One who loved him more than anyone.

Can't we all relate to Peter in some way? Jesus calls us out and gives us instructions, only for us to not listen. Maybe you knew you weren't supposed to have sex with that person but, in the moment, you didn't think it would matter. As soon as it was over, you felt anger, shame, and like you let Jesus down. Or, could it possibly be that you have allowed no margin for God to work in your life? You are trying to control it all instead of surrendering it to Him.

By the world's definition it would appear as though you have failed many times over, making you nothing more than a failure. You make a mistake and the world calls you a failure, so you give up, hide, run, and ask, "What's the point?"

I want us to pay attention to and learn from the way Peter handled his emotions after betraying Jesus. Did Peter run and hide? Did Peter give up? More on that in just a little bit.

## You Have Two Options

I have talked a lot about Peter, but now I want to talk about Judas, his betrayal, and how he handled his emotions. Just like Jesus told Peter that he would deny Him three times, Jesus knew that Judas was going to betray Him as well. Matthew 26:21–25 says:

*While they were eating, he said, "I tell you the truth, one of you will betray me." Greatly distressed, each one asked in turn, "Am I the one, Lord?" He replied, "One of you who has just eaten from this bowl with me will betray me. For the Son of Man must die, as the Scriptures declared long ago. But how terrible it will be for the one who betrays him. It would be far better for that man if he had never been born!" Judas, the one who would betray him, also asked, "Rabbi, am I the one?" And Jesus told him, "You have said it."*

Judas asks if he is the one to betray Jesus. What a bold question. It wasn't until Satan entered Judas that he would then begin his betrayal for some extra money on the side. Luke 22:2–6 tells us how Judas' betrayal began:

*The leading priests and teachers of religious law were plotting how to kill Jesus, but they were afraid of the people's reaction.*

*Then Satan entered Judas Iscariot, who was one of the twelve disciples, and he went to the leading priests and captains of the Temple guard to discuss the best way to betray Jesus to them. They were delighted, and they promised to give him money. So, he agreed and began looking for an opportunity to betray Jesus so they could arrest him when the crowds weren't around.*

Judas would show the Chief Priests who Jesus was by kissing Him on the cheek. *His betrayer had given them a sign: "The One I kiss, He's the One; arrest Him!" So, he went right up to Jesus and said, "Greetings, Rabbi!" and kissed Him* (Matthew 26:48–49). Did Judas really understand what was happening? So many emotions here, right? It's easy for us to say that we would never do that to Him. We know what happens, though. We know how the story ends. Judas doesn't. Peter didn't. Jesus did.

Peter and Judas both betrayed Jesus in some way. So many of us may have experienced it, too (or keep re-experiencing it), by living in the past. Shame consumes us. Guilt makes us want to hide. Condemnation keeps us from experiencing His mercy and His grace. Although Peter and Judas both betrayed Jesus, they had very different endings in the way that they dealt with their emotions and betrayal.

Let's look at how Judas handled everything first, in Matthew 27:3–5:

*When Judas, who had betrayed him, realized that Jesus had been condemned to die, he was filled with remorse. So, he took the thirty pieces of silver back to the leading priests and the elders. "I have sinned," he declared, "for I have betrayed an innocent man."*

*"What do we care?" they retorted. "That's your problem." Then Judas threw the silver coins down in the Temple and went out and **hanged himself.***

Judas felt so much pain from the betrayal and knew that it couldn't be fixed, so he hanged himself. Jesus wasn't even on the cross yet. Judas took matters into his own hands. Judas created his own punishment for what he had done. Judas turned to himself to find the answers. Judas gave himself the death he thought he deserved.

Many of you right now are punishing yourself for something, something you have done or something that has been done to you. You have created your own terms for the punishment and what you think you deserve. You are trying to make up your own rules. You have decided that *this* (whatever it is) is your only option, so you will choose to stay there. You are saying that what Jesus did on the cross wasn't enough and that you don't deserve it—that you aren't worth the price He paid.

How did Peter handle his emotions and betrayal? We are going to get to that, but first I want to point out one more thing: what happened when the Sabbath was over. When the Sabbath was over and Mary Magdalene; Mary, the mother of James; and Salome went to the tomb, a young man dressed in a white robe said to them, "But go, tell *His disciples* **and Peter**, 'He is going ahead of you into Galilee. There you will see him, just as he told you.'" (See Mark 16:1–7.) Jesus, thank you for not forgetting about us when we have gone astray and left the shelter of your wings. They were instructed to go tell His disciples and Peter, almost saying that Peter wouldn't be considered a disciple because he denied Him. His love continues regardless of our human error and regardless of what we feel. What He feels about us often looks quite different from how we feel about us. That Jesus still claimed Peter as His own meant that the resurrection was also Peter's salvation.

I love reading about the third encounter with His disciples in John 21:4–8:

*Just as day was breaking, **Jesus stood on the shore**; yet the disciples did not know that it was Jesus. Jesus said to them, "**Children**, do you have any fish?" They answered him, "No." He said to them, "Cast the net on the right side of the boat, and you will find some." So, they cast it, and now they were not able to haul it in, because of the quantity of fish. That disciple whom Jesus loved therefore said to Peter, "It is the Lord!" **When Simon Peter heard that it was the Lord, he put on his outer garment, for he was stripped for work, and threw himself into the sea.** The other disciples came in the boat, dragging the net full of fish, for they were not far from the land, but about a hundred yards off.*

Despite the pain, regrets, shame, and so many other emotions that Peter would be feeling at the time, he decided to go fishing. Something he knew. Something he was used to. Maybe falling into his old ways because of what was going on inside of him? (Sound familiar, anyone?) What I love most about this encounter is that He addresses them as His children. He stood on the shore, blessed their fishing trip with an abundance of fish (especially since they had been fishing all night and were probably exhausted), and then called them in and they had breakfast together. Can we just take a moment to note how Peter responded after he knew it was Jesus? He threw himself into the sea. He didn't care about anything else happening around him. He had his eyes set on his Father and he swam in about a hundred yards. Meanwhile, the rest came back with the boat and the fish. Peter was His child. Peter knew He was his Father. Let that just sink in for a moment. Picture what it really would have looked like. I imagine it would be like you being gone from your children for a few days and then, when you walk in the door, they come screaming, "Mommy! Daddy!" That's how He wants us to enter His presence. He is our Daddy and we are His children. Peter failed forward right in his Father's arms.

Shortly after breakfast together, Jesus asked Peter three times if Peter loved Him, and every time Peter said, "You know that I love you." (Isn't it like the Father's love that Peter denied Him three times and Jesus asked him three times?) This encounter is more instruction about what will be to come of Peter and the kind of death that Peter will have to glorify God. (See John 21:15–19.)

In the Book of Acts we read what Peter does after the coming of the Holy Spirit. To keep it short, he gave a killer sermon at Pentecost and "three thousand souls were saved" (Acts 2:41).

## Failure Isn't Final

Here's the deal: There will be many times when you will want to give up, throw in the towel, and strive to be normal. Sometimes being the light He has called us to be requires us to be uncomfortable and feel vulnerable most of the time. I could have given up when I failed the test. I could have given up when I dropped out of college twice. I could have given up many times in between. The problem I see the most is that when something doesn't go the way you thought it should, then you quit altogether and check yourself off as a failure. You tried something once, so it must not be for you or from God. Then you convince yourself that everything you ever did that was a mistake caused your failure, and you don't think you deserve to have success, and so God is punishing you for it. Then you begin to live the rest of your life in prison—a prison that He never once called you to live in, placed you in, or said you ever had to go to.

You know what happens when you try to create your own prison for punishment. We have already discussed that. What you need to focus on is getting yourself out of the prison you keep putting yourself in. Here are a few questions to ask yourself:

1. What or who made me feel like I don't deserve God's love, grace, and mercy in my life?
2. Am I more connected to His word on a regular basis, or am I more connected with the world and what it says I should feel?
3. What am I trying to prove by putting myself in prison?

4. Does what I feel abide with His word?
5. Have I truly forgiven and repented the things of my past, or am I still trying to hold on?

When something doesn't go the way you thought it would, can we agree that you learned a lot during the process? It's easy to look at the things that didn't go right as failures but they're really invitations and opportunities. An opportunity to try it again but a little differently. An opportunity to discover more of the things you love and more of the things you dislike. An invite to step closer to who He is and His purpose for you. An invite that says, "You are doing great things. Keep going and keep pressing on toward the prize." I have tried many things on this crazy adventure with Him and I know I will continue to try things if I am open to receiving and willing to step into that space.

Let right now be your opportunity and invite. It's time for action, my friend. It's time to unlock the door to the prison you have yourself in and let our God, who is a chain-breaker, break those chains off you. This isn't something you are going to work for. This is something you receive.

Get yourself ready. Open the palms of your hands. No more fists. Be still and be quiet. No more striving. No more prison. You are an heir. You are His daughter, His child. Close your eyes and picture yourself as one running to a Father who is smiling and with His arms wide open just waiting to scoop you into them.

## Chapter 2
## The Stealer of My Peace

≡

I woke up and did my morning routine, which usually consists of some sort of hot tea, a shake, foam rolling, and drinking at least 30 ounces or so of water. I sat down to journal, to read, and to enjoy a slow Monday morning. (My husband was home, which always causes me to have slower mornings, so I have learned to embrace the slow.) After a little while, I grabbed my phone and opened my social media apps. I usually check Instagram first and then Facebook. In a matter of 15 minutes, I realized I had lost myself in all the posts and I could feel my mood change. The time I spent just before opening my social media apps was peaceful. There wasn't anything rushing me, telling me to do more or do something different, and there wasn't anything in my face saying I should eat a better breakfast than the shake I just had.

In a blink of any eye, I allowed social media to take my joy. To convince me of all the things I wasn't doing right or could do better. I *let* it make me feel like I wasn't enough. My food wasn't good enough. My prayer time wasn't spent right. Maybe I should have worked out at 7 a.m., too? All these questions of what I should do different the next morning, what I should eat different, and how I could be different surfaced. Just like that, I went from believing in Him calling me good to me telling myself, "You can do better, Jess." All of this led me to want to shrug my shoulders forward and get right to work to change everything.

This morning was different, though. After spending that short amount of time on social media, I refused to let it take my joy yet again. I wanted this time to be different. I wanted to return home—back to the place where He calls me good. I wanted to figure out why I allowed it to steal my joy. Instead of just accepting it for what it is and instead of just accepting the thoughts that came to me, I wanted an answer.

I grabbed my journal, which was right next to my phone, and started to write. I have been journaling more than I usually do lately, and a bunch of lies that I have believed for so long have been surfacing. Lies that have been attached to an outcome that I was letting define who I was, how good I was, and how much value I hold; things I didn't realize I was holding onto. I never wanted to slow down enough to simply ask Him to show me more. Comparison that led me out of sync with my Creator and that tried to tell me everyone else's life is and was better than mine because of the broken pieces in my own life.

I wrote in my journal, "There is something defeating about social media that sits in my spirit and I really need to work on why and then step into freedom." I continued to write, "It makes me feel like my life isn't as good. That I am not a good writer or that I could be a better writer." There I was, writing to Him exactly how I felt when I logged into social media. It was true how I felt. But, like Alisa Keeton, author and ministry owner of Revelation Wellness, writes in her book *The Wellness Revelation*, "Feelings are meant to be felt, not drive what we do." (Preach!) Alisa continues to write, "Give humans something good, and they have to have more. If a little is good, then a lot must be better, right?" The next thing Alisa writes was one of my biggest revelations between spirit and flesh I have had: "The flesh never knows when to say when. Left to its own reasoning, the flesh always says, 'More!'"

## Oh, My Flesh

Why did I never make the connection before? *When I log in into my social media apps, my flesh is telling me more, not my spirit.* I continued to write in my journal and I continued to sit there longer, until I encountered peace. It wasn't going to happen unless I was intentional about making it happen and pursuing it. I was determined to not let 15 minutes of seeing amazing people in my feed let me feel like I wasn't good. (Yes, I said amazing people. I love the people I choose to follow. It was never about them. I'm sure you know what I am going to say next: It was about me.) Here's what came to me when I began to feel peace: *Jess, you are good.* I started to write a list of categories that stole my joy and peace. I wrote little things I felt like the Lord said were good to address. The feeling that I had to change all areas of life right away went away. I took a deep breath in, let it out, and opened my laptop to write to you, because I knew I couldn't be the only one who experiences this. I wanted to return home, back to His arms, and where I belong. He is calling the same for you. He wants all of you, not specific areas.

We cannot live on the sidelines of our life. Logging into social media and expecting it to make us feel good and fulfilled don't work. We can't leave the *"shelter of His wings"* (see Psalm 91:4) and not be intentional about where our thoughts go. He is with us, no doubt, but we must remain and abide in Him. We see this in John 15:4:

*Remain in me, as I also remain in you. No branch can bear fruit by itself; it must remain in the vine. Neither can you bear fruit unless you remain in me.*

He says that we cannot bear fruit unless we remain in Him. When we log into social media, we must remain in Him. His thoughts toward us. Our posture toward Him. I can tell you for sure I was not bearing fruit by feeling as though I wasn't good. If I chose to stay in the posture that I wasn't good, then everything I did after that would flow out of that place (of not being good). How would that benefit you? How would that benefit me?

I'm not saying to get rid of all our apps. I'm not saying social media is bad. My business is 90% run on social media. (You probably wouldn't be reading this book if it wasn't for God's gift of the Internet.) I run an online member community called Own Your Worth, I am an online wholeness and wellness coach and a writer, and I use social media for whatever

I feel like the Lord is tugging at me to share next. You are probably in the same boat even if you are not an entrepreneur. There are things that you want to share but you just don't know how to share them. Mostly everything I do either involves a website or logging into one of my social media apps. It's a good thing when used right. I am not going to dive into a social media lesson here, but I want to make sure we check ourselves when it comes to social media. I have wrestled with both sides of this whole social media thing. Sometimes I feel like I retreat because of the thoughts that I do have, so I go silent for a little while to correct and get myself refocused on what really matters. The other side is being on social media and not feeling peace within myself.

## Living Well

The two biggest questions I am faced with (and am assuming you are, too) are: (1) How can we use our social media presence for good without deflating ourselves and the life God has given us, and (2) What does this look like in our lives when we begin to live it out? If our goal is to return home (to the shelter of His wings) every time a thought comes in that doesn't align with His truth, then we must create an atmosphere in our office, in our daily life, and within our phones themselves. This is when it's time for you to do the work—the deep work that is going to be uncomfortable and so against what the rest of the world may be doing. Following are three action steps I have put into place in my own life to redirect me back to home whenever I get lost. These steps take me back to the resting place and a place of peace. I may not do these all at once, but I do choose at least one to apply instantly, when I recognize my peace has been stolen.

**1. I pray for those I compare myself to.** I speak it out of my mouth, I tell it to my mind, and then it follows down into my heart. I started doing this a few short months ago when I realized it was happening. Not wanting the enemy to win, I lifted them higher. I commented on their post, liked their photo, or texted them personally. The women I find myself comparing myself to are amazing women. There is no room for comparison. There is, however, plenty of room in the Kingdom. Praying for others' success, families, and hearts takes the focus off me and what I (or think I) lack and raises someone else up. I don't know about you, but when I make someone else's day by a simple act of kindness, it completely changes my heart.

We see a perfect example of this in Paul's letter in Philippians 2:3–4:

*Do nothing out of selfish ambition or vain conceit. Rather, in humility value others above yourselves, not looking to your own interests but each of you to the interests of the others.*

That is teaching us the humility of Jesus. Nowhere does it say that we should devalue ourselves to raise others up. We are to stand firm in who we are in Him, but our goal and mission are not about us. I am not claiming perfection here. Comparison still creeps in, but at least I have something in place that I know I can go to for instant peace (and now so do you).

**2. I close out of the app and turn off my phone.** (I also shut off my phone at night or leave it in another room. It doesn't go to bed with me, and I don't wake up checking it.) I check my phone for no reason at all throughout the day. As I scroll I even catch myself saying, "Why am I on here?" I then close the app and turn off my phone. When I turn off my phone, I hold it in my hand and say a short prayer, something like: "God, I don't want this to define any part of me. I know you see my heart and will bless my obedience. You will make things happen whether I am on my phone or not. Let this be a tool for my mission and nothing more."

Does that make your skin crawl at all? Do you get a little uncomfortable when you turn off your phone? When my phone is off, I do not check it nearly as much. Then when I *do* check after it has been off for a while, I'm reminded that I didn't miss out on too much of anything.

This is violent acts against the flesh. The flesh is going to try to tell you that you might miss out on something, so you better keep your phone on. You *"must give up your own way so that He can live through you"* (see Luke 9:23–24). We reach for our phones when standing in line, sitting in our cars, watching TV, eating, and the list goes on. Our phones fill the gap for when there may be opportunity for silence.

**3. I spend time journaling.** Have you journaled and spent time exploring the broken pieces in your life that make you feel less than when on social media? I've mentioned journaling many time before because I am that passionate about it. When you have nothing but a piece of paper and a pen, things can come up that you didn't know existed.

I have discovered so much about myself when I just let the words flow onto a piece of paper, no matter what they were. Anger. Sadness. Jealousy. Confusion. Joy. Whatever it is that comes to my mind, I write it down. I don't have music playing in the background. I don't have my Bible out for reference. When I need to do a serious brain release I sit there in silence and write. I don't try to think of something good to say or what I think He wants to hear. I just let it keep flowing and coming out. We need to be more honest with ourselves. We need to spend more time grieving how we feel.

Paul wrote in 2 Corinthians 7:10, *"For Godly grief produces a repentance that leads to salivation without regret, whereas world grief produces death."* We have been told for so long to just move on, and that God is good and He'll bring something better. (I know I have said this myself.) While all those statements are true, I believe we are missing one part of it all: When we try to move on without ever letting our feelings or emotions rise so that we can grieve them with Him, it can cause a downward spiral of emotions later. (This is a reason why we compare and never feel good enough when opening our social media apps.) It's okay to feel what you feel if you don't stay there. Grieving with Him produces life. Forgetting what you feel and brushing it under the rug only lead to bitterness and resentment later (or death, as Paul would say at the end of 2 Corinthians 7:10).

If you are someone who doesn't really journal, is just beginning to journal, or wants to journal, I want to share a few tips that can help you!

**1. Find a space where you feel comfortable to write.** Find a space where you can focus and concentrate. Don't overthink this.

**2. Ask yourself questions.** If you are ever unsure of what to write, ask yourself questions. It helps you to reflect on the day or week you have had. For example: *What happened today? How did it make me feel?*

**3. Time yourself.** It's easy to get lost in writing sometimes. Setting a timer for 10 minutes to start with can help you stay focused and productive, especially if you're new to journaling.

**4. Date your entry.** Don't forget to put a date down on the paper whenever you begin to write. There is nothing better than going back through your journals to see where you were on specific days and how far you have come.

**5. Write honestly.** Write as if no one will ever see what you have written. Don't lie to yourself. That doesn't help you. Journaling can be very therapeutic. A lot of self-discovery can happen when you are open and honest with what's going on inside.

**6. Write quickly.** Don't give yourself time to think about it. Just let the words flow and see what kind of writing follows.

**7. Write naturally.** Let your thoughts come to paper. Don't worry if they are all out of order and all over the place. (This isn't an English paper!)

I love this scripture from Proverbs 4:10:

*Dear friend, take my advice; it will add years to your life. I'm writing out clear directions to Wisdom Way, I'm drawing a map to Righteous Road. I don't want you ending up in blind alleys, or wasting time making wrong turns. Hold tight to good advice; don't relax your grip. Guard it well—your life is at stake. Don't take Wicked Bypass; don't so much as set foot on that road. Stay clear of it; give it a wide berth. Make a detour and be on your way.*

Where should our hearts be? Where should we have our focus? On all things that are good, pure, and edifying. Yet, our flesh is usually wired to think the opposite. Let's guard our peace well.

## Sitting and Silence

Yesterday I was at the hair salon. I wanted something new and different, so I knew the appointment would take longer than unusual upon arrival. Lately I have been challenged by some people in my life (whom I admire greatly) to create more margin for the good stuff, more silence, and more of the *"be still and know I am God"* (Psalm 46:10) kind of sitting. I am pretty sure I am the only woman I know who doesn't really enjoy getting her hair done. There is something about sitting there for two-plus hours that never really got me excited. Enjoying time with my friend who does my hair is always nice, but the process was always tedious and mundane. Tori, my hair stylist, knows I would rather walk out the door with wet hair at the end than to sit there even longer for her to blow dry my hair (especially when I am just going home anyway!).

This visit was different, because I was determined to just sit and enjoy being there and not dread the sitting part. Trying to find something to fill the time, I would pick up my phone. Why? I have no clue. I already did everything I needed to do on it. "Be with Me" are a few words I keep hearing from Him lately. I would put the phone down. I would sit in silence that lasted less than five minutes. Then I would pick up my book and begin to read. After a few pages, I would hear the words again: "Be with Me." We (meaning He and I) went back and forth with each other the whole time I was there, which was roughly three hours. As you can tell, I am a work in progress.

I have missed so much of my life because I have been so busy looking down at my phone trying to be noticed that I wasn't noticing what was happening around me. I would try to fill any empty space in my life with something. My phone was my outlet to fill the space. It saddens my heart to think I have missed out on some of my husband's conversations with me because I was looking down instead of at him. It breaks my heart to think that anyone in my life would feel second to my phone.

Then this extremely tough question came from Him: "Do you know who you are, what you like, what you enjoy, what makes you laugh, when you are just with you, Jess?" He continued, "If someone were to ask you what you love to do for fun, could you answer?" Oh boy, I could honestly say I didn't know. Let me ask the question to you: Do you know who you are, what you like, what you enjoy, what makes you laugh, when you are just with you and Him? I wasn't aware of how far down the rabbit hole I had gone. I turned 30 while writing this book and I felt like I had to start over from the beginning. Work was my life. Fitness was my life. My phone was my lifeline to all of that. Who was I?

## This Is Who You Are

We have lost who we are and most of us don't even know. We are walking around trying to live in someone else's word from the Lord, gifts, talents, and purpose. It's easy to open our social media apps and feel like we are missing something if we don't try the latest this and that. It's a constant striving and a constant pursuit that we will by our flesh and that tells us there is more to be done.

When the Lord asked me what I enjoy and what I love to do that doesn't involve work or fitness, I had to do some deep work to begin to figure it out. A lot more sitting and writing in my journal occurred. More than usual. I also took some action by buying a camera because I always enjoyed photography growing up.

I wanted to share a few truths about who we are in Him.

## We Are His Friends
*I no longer call you slaves, because the slave does not understand what his master is doing. But I have called you friends, because I have revealed to you everything I heard from my Father.*
(John 15:15)

## We Are Not Condemned
*There is therefore now no condemnation for those who are in Christ Jesus.*
(Romans 8:1)

## We Are Fearfully Made
*You are fearfully and wonderfully made.*
(Psalm 139:14)

## We Are His Children
*In Christ Jesus you are all children of God through faith.*
(Galatians 3:26)

## We Are New
*Therefore, if anyone is in Christ, the new creation has come: The old has gone, the new is here!*
(2 Corinthians 5:17)

## We Are His Masterpiece
*For we are God's masterpiece. He has created us anew in Christ Jesus, so we can do the good things he planned for us long ago.*
(Ephesians 2:10)

## We Are Forgiven
*But if we confess our sins to him, he is faithful and just to forgive us our sins and to cleanse us from all wickedness.*
(1 John 1:9)

## We Are a Royal Priesthood and His Prized Possession
*But you are a chosen people, a royal priesthood, a holy nation, God's special possession, that you may declare the praises of him who called you out of darkness into his wonderful light.*
(1 Peter 2:9)

## We Are Free
*Now the Lord is the Spirit, and where the Spirit of the Lord is, there is freedom.*
(2 Corinthians 3:17)

The problem we face is that the constant pursuit and constant striving to find who we are are usually spent trying to find it in something, not Someone. I believe most of us know what He says about us but have an extremely hard time believing He could feel that way. This is why we hope that something else will give us the feelings that we crave: to be seen, heard, and loved. There is no room for His love when our entire body is filled with pain, hurt, anger, jealousy, comparison, and everything else you can think of that brings no fruit to our lives.

I think the question we should ask ourselves is: How do we take back what has already been given to us, a *"spirit that gives us power, does not make us timid, gives us love, and self-disci-*

*pline"* (see 2 Timothy 1:7)? I think it begins with calling out by name things that have stolen your peace. For example: *I will not be controlled by what other people say. I will not allow money to be number one in my marriage anymore.*

We must begin to speak out bold statements that have consumed our hearts for so long that the worry has begun to dry rot our hearts and that have caused us to slowly die inside over time. Write them all down. Write down as many as you can possibly think of. Whatever comes up, write it down. Get it out. Stop holding it in. Stop letting it run over in your mind like a movie that never stops playing and the ending only gets worse each time. For every area and for every sentence you wrote, go to His word and put the truth right next to it. What does God say about that problem? What does God say about this area of your life? What is He telling you about these feelings that you feel? If we want to get our peace back, we must be violent about the war we are fighting. Stop fighting with your husband, friends, and family, because the war isn't with them.

This assignment is not a "one and done" kind of assignment, either. Luke 6:45 says:

*A good man brings good things out of the good stored up in his heart, and an evil man brings evil things out of the evil stored up in his heart. For the mouth speaks what the heart is full of.*

Everything we say and do stems from what is in our hearts. I am a firm believer that the world will only begin to change when we begin to change ourselves from the inside out. So much (too much) energy is spent trying to change other people around us that we neglect ourselves. Really, the work needs to be done on us first. It's nearly impossible to love your neighbor when you can't say one nice thing about yourself, or when every word that comes out of your mouth speaks of anger, jealousy, bitterness, lack, and more. Behind every person are pain and hurt that we know nothing about. The second commandment in the Bible says to "love your neighbor as yourself." It's one of the hardest for us to live out in our daily lives, especially when, in a matter of a few seconds, we can pick up our phones and instantly begin to pick ourselves apart with comparison.

Living out who we are will look like nothing this world has to offer. If you have lost your peace, just like I did and will still do, then it's time to set yourself up for Kingdom success. Not the success that tells you that you are doing well because of how many likes and followers you have, but rather the kind of success that makes you ask these questions: Is it worthy of Jesus? Is it loving? Is it unifying?

## Kingdom Success Principles

Since we are on the topic of success, I want to share with you a few foundational pieces that you can begin to live out every day to really help you define what success may look like to you. You will hear a lot of talk about purpose, mission, vision, and passion when it comes to success, so that is what we will be discussing. When we realize we are worth more than the only thing we know to be true no matter what happens in our life—that God is greater and bigger than anything and we are not what we do—we are who we are because of Him.

For a long time (and occasionally it still likes to rear its ugly head) success meant how much I had, how many followers I gained, or how much money I made. Anything that a number could be attached to, that's where I put my identity and my success. By the world's standards, when you continue to add items to your "everything I have done and accomplished" list, the more successful you are. That can make many of us feel not so successful when we begin to base our success on what we see others achieving. I always like to note that none of those things are bad—unless, of course, we make them our idol, our savior, and the source of our joy and happiness. I believe our God is an abundant God and He is the one who created wealth. I want to make sure that your focus is on the main thing. I have chased everything under the sun, and none of felt really fulfilling because I always wanted more or because what I had was never good enough.

Let's look at Psalm 37:4–7, in which we find key foundational Kingdom principles to live by when it comes to defining success and how you choose to live your life (and who you live your life for):

***Take delight in the Lord****, and He will give you the desires of your heart.* ***Commit your way to the Lord****;* ***trust in Him*** *and He will do this: He will make your righteous reward shine like the dawn, your vindication like the noonday sun.* ***Be still before the Lord****, and wait patiently for Him: do not fret when people succeed in their ways, when they carry out their wicked schemes.*

Psalm 37:4 starts us off with instruction to *"**take delight in the Lord and He will give you the desires of your heart.**"* This scripture goes along with our purpose: to take delight in Him. So many of us think the more we praise Him the more we will get the things we want. Our praise shouldn't be about *what* we get but *Who* we get. He will give us our desires, but what we want and what He wants for us always looks different. You might feel like your life just got destroyed, but I can tell you that sometimes the things that He takes away, or that we feel like He takes away, or when we feel like our heart's been broken, often are blessings in disguise. We can't even see it because we can't even wrap our heads around how much He loves us. More than anything, He looks out for our safety and sometimes is protecting us. So, when it comes to success, a great question to ask is: Whatever is in my heart that is not aligned with Your will, then take it away. Yes, ask Him for whatever desire you may have, but also ask Him to take away what isn't a part of His will for your life. It's tough but so worth it.

The second instruction comes from Psalm 37:5: *"**Trust in Him and He will do this.**"* When it comes to passion it's a strong and barely controllable emotion to help people in some way, shape, or form. What does that uncontrollable emotion to help people look like for you? Passion is what gets our hearts stirring to do things bigger and greater than we could ever imagine. As that passions stirs, let's make sure you focus on trusting in the Lord. You are not to be ruled by fear. Fear will be there and try to make its attacks, but His love is greater.

The third instruction comes from Psalm 37:5 as well: *"**Com-mit** your way to the Lord."* When we talk about vision, it's about this: What do you want to become? When you close your eyes, what do you see? When was the last time you allowed yourself to dream past the money in your bank account and the situation you may be in right now? When you envision where you want to go, something extremely powerful happens deep within you. It's almost like you can begin to feel the feelings you would have as if the vision was already true. Being sure to make sure what we envision aligns with Him. Not running out before Him but committing your ways to Him. Surrender. Don't be afraid to dream with God.

If God has placed a passion on your heart and given you visions for it then Psalm 37:7 should also speak to you: *"**Be Still** before the Lord, and wait patiently for Him."* Your mission is an important assignment. It is not to be distracted or compared to. Maybe you have been dreaming for a long time but have told yourself it could never happen to you because you aren't lucky enough or smart enough. The excuses are endless, and every excuse you tell yourself only makes you believe the lie even more. (You know you can win any battle in your mind, right?) Being still doesn't mean you aren't productive. Being still before Him doesn't have to involve doing nothing. Yes, there are moments when we should be still and do nothing. But many times being still means to stop trying to jump out ahead of Him. Scripture tells us to wait patiently for Him. That's on His time, my friend. Be obedient in the time that you have and bring what's on your heart alive in that time, but don't rush ahead because you hate how slow it takes to build, grow, and learn.

If we are not taking delight, trusting, committing, or being still before the Lord, then what is all that you are going after really for, if it's not about Him or giving glory to Him? Tough question, I know, but a good one to constantly ask yourself when it comes to your goals and how you determine your success.

Remember who you are, but more importantly this is about remembering *whose* you are.

## Chapter 3
## Returning Home

Chris Tomlin wrote a song called "Home" that takes me back to my real home. That home is not on this earth.

I found myself trapped in a trailer that could barely fit four people, had barely any furniture, and was extremely dark and rather quiet. A man appeared dressed in black. He was a taller figure, and he had kept me there and threatened me. It wasn't so much his words that threatened me. I remember feeling afraid and threatened by the way he walked and stood there. It was a slow and steady walk, with his arms postured at his side. I was too afraid to leave. The place looked very familiar, but I didn't know where I was. My hands were roped together, and fear took over my body. *How am I going to get out? Will anyone know I am missing?* In my head, I began to plan my escape route and praying someone would save me and find me. The next thing I know, I saw clear blue skies and a big mansion in the distance, and I was sitting at a table taking it all in. The fear had passed, and I was experiencing freedom. It was warm outside, with those clear blue skies, compared to the dark trailer that felt cold and eerie. I sat at the table in awe of what I was seeing. *Is this real?* I asked. It was just enough to show me a little piece of heaven. Then I woke up.

I remember that dream very vividly. (It happened about three years ago.) It was as though I was trapped in my past and begging for someone to find me, love me, and rescue me all over again. Then the Lord picked me up out of that trailer and put me right on His lap to show me a different way and a different perspective. I was home—a home where I didn't have to worry. A home where I knew I belonged. A home that welcomed me regardless of what had happened to me or what I had done to others. That same morning, when I woke up from the dream, the Lord shared with me John 14:1–4:

*Do not let your hearts be troubled. You believe in God; believe also in me. My Father's house has many rooms; if that were not so, would I have told you that I am going there to prepare a place for you? And if I go and prepare a place for you, I will come back and take you to be with me that you also may be where I am. You know the way to the place where I am going.*

One translation reads: *"In my Father's house are many* **mansion***s: if it were not so, I would have told you. I go to prepare a place for you."*

Clear blue skies. Warmth. Freedom. Home. Heaven.

## Home Is Where Your Heart Is

Have you heard the phrase "Home is where your heart is"?

Such a funny saying, isn't it? But also so very true. When I hear that phrase, I think about the different places my home has been. My body. My business. My relationships. If home is where your heart is, can't we be honest enough to say to ourselves that our home hasn't always been wrapped up in a warm, cozy blanket, curled up next to a fireplace, in a place that has a number with a street name attached to it?

I will be the first in line to raise my hand to the fact that I have traveled a lot. I have gone from home to home trying to find one that is just right—one that is big enough, provides the right kind of safety, is part of a nice neighborhood, and makes me feel welcome. (I'm speaking hypothetically here, of course.)

I put down roots in my business and thought that this would be good for a long while. It felt right. Provided freedom. Things felt safe.

I put down roots in my body. This looked good. I had a good-looking yard and a white picket fence but felt alone and isolated from other people.

I put down roots in my relationships. I loved the community but hated the expectations. I loved the closeness of neighbors but was afraid to get too close to anyone.

There I would go again: moving onto another home for my heart. It's so exhausting to move, picking up all the pieces and putting them into boxes to carry into the next phase of my life. (I mean this literally, too.) I'm sure you know what happens when exhaustion kicks in? You throw your hands up, settle, and tell yourself you don't care what happens next. It becomes so overwhelming that you feel like you can barely manage to get out of bed to face the day. Yep, that was me.

*There must be something more than this,* I thought to myself often. This brings me to Matthew 11:28–30:

*Come to me, all you who are weary and burdened, and I will give you rest. Take my yoke upon you and learn from me, for I am gentle and humble in heart, and you will find rest for your souls. For my yoke is easy and my burden is light.*

We are going deep together with this one.

## Finding Home

In the current season of my life I have been craving and searching for more rest and peace. I wanted to feel home. See, after getting married, moving to a new state, leaving friends and family behind, leaving jobs and beginning news one, life events happening, and my health going in all different directions, I was craving home. A place to rest and kick up my feet after a long day's work. But see, my home (where I live) is my work. It's a blessing, yes! Just like anything, it always has its pros and cons. Working from home means I always see the laundry needing to be done, the dishes in the sink, the yard that needs tending to, the trash that needs taken out, the animals that need fed and taken care of, and an office that needs tending to. I have worked from home for about five years now. I have been able to keep up with all the work thus far because I have always been in a mental space of "If I don't do it, no one will." The hustle game lasted for a long time. Push harder. Work harder. Work smarter. Wake up early. Go to bed late. It never seemed to end for me. I was trying to do what others were doing. Home was never just a place to kick up my feet. Home was work.

My husband, Jon, can rest well. The dishes in the sink don't bother him. The clothes can sit in the dryer for a couple of days. The yard can wait. Vacuuming? Well, that can wait too. It's not that he doesn't care about things getting done. They are just not a higher level of importance to him at moments when he just wants to rest.

In the beginning of our marriage I would despise my husband. How dare he relax on the couch watching *Forensic Files*? Just sitting there, peacefully, enjoying one of his favorite shows. Meanwhile, I would be dusting, vacuuming, and frantically doing things "just to get them done." It's not that he didn't want to help. I often never asked; when I did, he would help. Often, I assumed he would see me and then just help. I wasn't communicating what was going on in my heart. I didn't really know why it made me so angry to see him relax when I wasn't. This whole story has nothing to do with Jon. This whole story is about me not knowing how to find rest.

It's not like the house was in a dire need of cleaning, either. It wasn't like I didn't wipe down the counters and dust the week before. But in my mind it needed to be done, and it needed to be done *now*. Jon would say, multiple times, "Why don't you ever just rest or slow down?" I would charge through with my declaration of "It needs to be done or else." Until one day, when we sat down to figure it out. Jon was the one who pointed out that it bothers me when I see him rest because I don't like to rest myself. Ouch! It was the truth, though. It bothered me that he could just sit there and enjoy his time watching one of his favorite shows and not really care about anything else. If I slowed down too long, then I would begin to think of everything that needed to be done or else I wouldn't be considered successful. Thoughts would race: *I need to return that email. I need to follow up with that person. I should probably text this person. Oh shoot, don't forget about that invite.* Everything from the outside world consumed my thoughts. Not too many thoughts stemmed from a place of "What is Jesus asking and telling me to do?"

I knew when Jon told me that, I had some work to do within myself. How can I be grounded and rooted in Christ and not grounded and rooted in what I do? Maybe the home I was searching for wasn't in a place but in a person?

## Getting Back to Your Roots

One morning before opening my eyes and getting out of bed I heard the Lord tell me, out of nowhere, that I was sanctified and He was the vinedresser. Every morning I try to say things I am grateful for and have small chats with God before getting out of bed, in that in-between when you are trying to wake up but haven't quite fully opened your eyes yet. I have begun to really claim that part of my morning as a starting place for my thoughts to be centered on Him.

I didn't have a clue what *sanctified* meant. It's not a word I heard too much or a word I ever used. So, of course, I Googled it. According to Google's dictionary, *sanctified* means "to purify, redeem, set apart as or declare holy." "Okay, Lord. you have my attention," I said. Then I Googled *vinedresser.* According to Google's dictionary, *vinedresser* means "person who trains, prunes, and cultivated vines." Put them together: God is our vinedresser and we are sanctified because of what Jesus did on the cross.

I continued to Google. I wanted to know what *holy* meant in biblical terms. *Holy:* "to be set apart or dedicated to God." It's a relationship that God desires with us. We can also think of holy as being pure. We are set apart for His service; to do His will for our lives.

*I will walk among you; I will be your God, and you will be my people.*
(Leviticus 26:12)

Even when He's pruning, ripping up weeds, and trimming off the extra, this doesn't change who we are. Even in the pain and mistakes and trials, we can rejoice because we are holy and pure and set apart. Pain doesn't mean He isn't good. Pain means He loves you so much to trim, rip up, and prune you to the life He's called you to live! We have almost trained ourselves to not feel our emotions but to be led by them without thought. It's easy to act on anger, but it's much harder to figure out where the anger came from in the first place. It's easy to ride the waves of our emotions, like coasting downstream in a river. It's a lot harder to pick up our raft and begin walking against the current to get back to where we started from.

When the Lord gave me those two words that morning He also took me right to John 15:1–8:

*I am the true vine, and My Father is the keeper of the vineyard. He cuts off every branch in Me that bears no fruit, and every branch that does bear fruit, He prunes to make it even more fruitful. You are already clean because of the word I have spoken to you. Remain in Me, and I will remain in you. Just as no branch can bear fruit by itself unless it remains in the vine, neither can you bear fruit unless you remain in Me.*

*I am the vine and you are the branches. The one who remains in Me, and I in him, will bear much fruit. For apart from Me you can do nothing. If anyone does not remain in Me, he is like a branch that is thrown away and withers. Such branches are gathered up, thrown into the fire, and burned. If you remain in Me and My words remain in you, ask whatever you wish, and it will be done for you. This is to My Father's glory, that you bear much fruit, proving yourselves to be My disciples.*

What is He saying? He is saying that He will, with toughness and tenderness, prune from us those things in our life that will not bear fruit. His pruning is to redirect us to a path that will bear fruit. If we don't lean on Him for the answers or the way in which we should go, then nothing we do will bear fruit. Can we still create what some would call success apart from Him? Sure. But, is that the kind of success you want? Self-seeking, self-glorifying success? I've done that for many years of my life, and the self-seeking success brings momentary joy and maybe some financial gain, but long term it's exhausting and a never-ending battle to be the next person "on top." I have watched people on my coaching team and inside my member community chase after temporary and fleeting emotions. In the end, isn't that what we are really chasing after anyway? Something to fill the brokenness, loneliness, and poorness in our spirits?

Asking for help from others is great, reading scripture is great, and quoting scripture is great, but something happens when you sit before Him as a child would with their father and let Him teach you His ways. Scripture tells us that Jesus went away to by himself to pray. It was quiet. He was going back to His roots, to the One who created Him. Luke 6:12 tells us about His quiet time: *"It was at this time that He went off to the mountain to pray, and He spent the whole night in prayer to God."* When was the last time you got quiet and just sat with Him? Not striving to fix something about you or your circumstance, but spent time with Him?

I have spent the last two months spending time with Him in quiet places. I walk without listening to podcasts or music. I sit and eat without checking my phone or turning on the TV. I simply ask Him to show me who He is and who I am. I am not striving to find an answer or guidance on which path to take. I simply say, "Here I am," and let Him tend to my heart. I have stripped down my business adventures so that He could show me what is most important and whom I have spent my time trying to be like. He's been tough. He's been tender. That's the heart of the Father. We must be willing to be pruned and for it to not look glamorous or for it to produce worldly results. We must be brave enough to fight the temptations to shut down and put an iron cage around our hearts. We must have the courage to stop pointing the finger and allow issues in our hearts to be dealt with.

## The In-Between

Children don't really understand lack or poverty, do they? When we were kids, our opinions formed by how our parents talked and acted based on what they felt. Our opinions formed because we heard and witnessed their opinions, whether good or bad. We don't know what we don't know, right? We submit to our parents because they raise us and lead us. We depend on them for safety, food, shelter, and knowledge. He asks us to change and become as little children before Him. Matthew 18:3 says: *And he said: "Truly I tell you, unless you change and become like little children, you will never enter the kingdom of heaven."*

He is looking for us to become like little children: to be humble, teachable, and trusting. For Him to be the One we run to for safety, food, shelter, and knowledge (wisdom). I love the one word in Google's definition of *childlike*: unworldly. Not corrupted, not trying to be like, not trying to pretend, but wanting to resemble their Father's actions and love.

How does this look in our everyday life? Well, slaves know how to work, and children know how to play, have fun, rest, and not worry about what is coming next. Most of us are slaves to our jobs, slaves to our bodies, slaves to what we do. We all know how to work. We know how to get things done. Deadlines, schedules, meetings, and more consume our time and energy with very little (if any) time for play. So that we can enter into His presence as a child, with a humble heart, knowing that we don't know it all, will never know it all, can't do it all, won't ever be able to do it all but that He is enough and all that we need.

In the midst of your everyday life of taking care of yourself, your husband, or your children, go to Him and just be with Him. (You are still with Him even when you are with someone else.) Maybe this looks like playing with your children versus worrying about the never-ending to-do list. Maybe it looks like enjoying the company of your husband and laughing together. Maybe it's making it a point to not have serious conversations in your play time with your husband. Maybe it looks like you being with yourself and doing things that you enjoy without the rules that you need to produce something. If you are single, this might look like going out into the world not afraid of being alone, and saying yes to hanging out with couples because you have no insecurity of being a third wheel. Enjoy life with Jesus without the feelings that you are not enough.

Paul wrote to the church in Colossae, *"Let your roots grow down into him, and let your lives be built on him. Then your faith will grow strong in the truth you were taught, and you will overflow with thankfulness"* (Colossians 2:7). Getting back to our roots—our real roots—will remind us of who we really are and who He really is.

## Ripping Up Weeds

At the beginning of summer, I set out on a mission to weed the flower beds outside of our windows and around our townhouse. Gardening—anything to do with gardening—brings me no joy. Zero. Nada. It's just one of those tasks that I don't get excited about. It takes me days to get the energy to go out there and rip up some weeds. (Maybe I am exaggerating a little bit, but still, it's not my favorite thing to do.) My husband knows this, so I set out to make him proud one day. I put on some gardening gear, grabbed one glove (because that's all I could find), and went outside to rip out some weeds. Thirty minutes was how long it took me to before I got bored and gave up. "Honey, look," I said. "I ripped up some weeds today"—as if I should be proud of the fact that I ripped up some weeds for 30 minutes and decided to let the rest of them grow out of control because, well, I just didn't feel like doing more.

What do you know? The next week the weeds I ripped up grew back but in different spots, and the ones I didn't even bother to rip up grew taller, larger, and wider until none of the flowers could be seen. I'm just thankful you can't see them now and you are only reading about them (although I am sure you can imagine what the mess the weeds have made outside of our townhouse). I know the potential of what it *could* look like, yet I just haven't bothered to clean it up and get rid of what doesn't belong. Zero motivation to go out there and do something that I just don't want to do.

Isn't this a beautiful picture, though, of what we do to ourselves within? We spend some time with God, ask Him to do wonders and miracles in our lives, but then we slowly just get too busy or too tired to check back in. Then, when things seem to get out of control again, we check back in ask Him to do some more work in our lives—and we go right back to being too busy or too tired to check in. It's a vicious cycle that's on repeat, one that needs to stop before you end up saying to yourself, "How did I end up here?" and "When did this get out of control like this?"

I believe that inside of us is a beautiful garden with every color imaginable. A garden filled with colors we don't even know exist that are saved just for us in heaven. Then in the middle of this beautiful garden are weeds—things that don't belong. It doesn't make the garden ugly. It doesn't make the garden less able to produce fruit. But if it goes on too long before the weeds are uprooted (not just trimmed or stepped on to get them out of the way), then the weeds will only begin to multiply.

When areas of insecurity, doubt, unbelief, shame, and whatever else that has taken root in your life goes unattended, what begins to happen? It begins to grow even more—until your everyday moments, conversations, relationships, and business adventures become one big root of fear that stems into your insecurity, doubt, unbelief, and shame. I have the honor of talking with many women who are inside the Own Your Worth Member Community (a community where wholeness and wellness meet God's word for women who want to experience freedom plus breakthroughs in Christ with food, body image, and relationships), and fear is the number-one thing that tends to hold them back. Fear of what others will think. Fear of failure. Fear they will be alone forever. All this fear, when you go back to the root cause, stems from a conversation or incident that made them feel one of the emotions we listed above. As author Hannah Anderson writes in her book *Humble Roots*, "We often mistake our emotional unsettledness as simply taking advantage of our difficult circumstances. As a result, we justify our short tempers and agitation because we are 'under stress.' We convince ourselves that our worry is normal because we have so much responsibility. And we end up treating the symptoms and not the root cause." Hannah continues, "We do not resolve our emotional uncertainty—our stress and anxiety—by focusing on our emotions themselves. We resolve the uncertainty by getting to the root cause. We resolve it by learning from Jesus."

Those emotions have been left unattended and to fend for themselves, which has allowed the enemy to use them as a weakness in your life and bring it to the front of your mind, making it seem like it is true and the most important thing for you to focus on. This, in the end, is why you can never seem to get past it: because you keep leaving it unattended. Jeremiah 24:7 is a beautiful scripture:

*I will give them a heart to know Me, for I am the LORD; and they will be My people, and I will be their God, for they will return to Me with their whole heart.*

Our heart is created to know Him, to want more of Him, and to love Him. As we mature in the Lord we realize all the things we try to put in His sacred place fail us. You could have all the money, perfect relationships, and an amazing body, and still feel like a piece is missing. That piece is Him. He's the piece of the puzzle that belongs in your life. You have been trying so hard and striving every day to fit that square peg in the round hole.

It's time to tend your garden. It's time to tend the weeds that have been overgrown for way too long. I know you are busy. You have a to-do list that is a mile long (and may include kids and/or a husband needing attention), and your quiet times seems to be slipping because you are just too busy.

It's easy to get into this too-busy lifestyle. We find routine. Things seem to be smooth sailing; we're coasting along. Then—bam—something happens that interrupts your day and completely wrecks your world emotionally. Suddenly, you found time for quiet time because you needed it, since it felt like someone or something poked a hole in your inner tube that stopped you from coasting along.

Now the emotions you kept at bay–all the insecurities, shame, or guilt–have come to the surface in one situation. Maybe it reminds you of something from your past and you get angry.

Maybe it reminds you of something that makes you cry because it's too painful.

Where am I going with this?

It will take time to work through and rip up those deep roots. Don't use time as your excuse. You must work on healing in that time. Time will pass (like it has) but if you don't do the inner work yourself, time won't make it go away. Inside the Own Your Worth Member Community, I challenge members with this, and I have been challenging myself as well. You'll need to make time for your quiet time, because you now know how important this is. Make it non-negotiable, even if it's just five minutes. If you want to stop lashing out, getting angry all time, and carrying pain from your past, then you will begin to go to Him more and more.

Our goal is not independence. Our goal is dependence—dependence on Him.

I have created a writing exercise for you. Get a pen and a piece of paper. On the blank piece of paper, begin writing down whatever you feel in the moment. Write whatever is bothering you or on your heart. (You can time yourself if you would like, but don't get caught up in rules of what something should be or look like.) After you've spent some time writing, write out a question you would like an answer to. After you write out the question, be still and wait until you hear an answer.

Don't try to force an answer. Just write whatever comes to your mind first. If you don't hear anything, try again tomorrow. This is about letting Him speak to you and you being quiet enough to listen. He has begun to show me so many things that I never really understood before. He has been showing me a new way—His way. I believe He is going to do the same for you!

One more thing I want to share is about the parable that Jesus shares about the sower. Let's look at Matthew 13:3–9 first:

*Then he told them many things in parables, saying: "A farmer went out to sow his seed. As he was scattering the seed, some fell along the path, and the birds came and ate it up. Some fell on rocky places, where it did not have much soil. It sprang up quickly, because the soil was shallow. But when the sun came up, the plants were scorched, and they withered because they had no root. Other seed fell among thorns, which grew up and choked the plants. Still other seed fell on good soil, where it produced a crop—a hundred, sixty or thirty times what was sown. Whoever has ears, let them hear."*

Then, in Matthew 13:18–23, He explains what it all means:
*Listen then to what the parable of the sower means: When anyone hears the message about the kingdom and does not understand it, the evil one comes and snatches away what was sown in their heart. This is the seed sown along the path. The seed falling on rocky ground refers to someone who hears the word and at once receives it with joy. But since they have no root, they last only a*

*short time. When trouble or persecution comes because of the word, they quickly fall away. The seed falling among the thorns refers to someone who hears the word, but the worries of this life and the deceitfulness of wealth choke the word, making it unfruitful. But the seed falling on good soil refers to someone who hears the word and understands it. This is the one who produces a crop, yielding a hundred, sixty or thirty times what was sown.*

Where are your roots being planted? Or better yet, what kind of soil are you trying to plant in?

## Chapter 4
## Mediocre

≡

My top love language is being outside. My husband knows and my friends know that if it is a sunny day, I am ready to go for a walk, go golfing, play tennis, go hiking—really anything that gets me outside where the sun beats down on my skin and my feet are in the grass and in nature.

The problem with wanting to do anything is that I was never great at one thing. When I played basketball in high school, I was way better at defense than offense. Dribbling a ball down the court scared me and I was extremely insecure about it. When I played indoor and outdoor soccer it was the same; I was way better at defense than offense. In my eyes, I was only good at half of a sport. (Or maybe even a quarter.) It was always that I was too short for this or not good enough at that. I enjoy playing tennis, but for the life of me I can barely return the ball without it going over the person's head (or, even better, almost over the fence).

I have been this way for as long as I can remember. I just love being able to move my body and playing sports; being active outside has just always rejuvenated me and made me come alive. God, why did you give me all these passions to play sports, be outside, rollerblade, and more if I am only half-good or a quarter-good? (Maybe you have asked God a similar question before?)

## The Lie

It was a beautiful sunny day. My husband and I try to take full advantage of sunny summer days here in Pennsylvania whenever we can. Jon, my husband, loves to play golf. I love to golf, too, but not as much as he does. Jon's goal is to play on the senior tour one day; my goal is to go out, have fun, and enjoy the sunshine. I guess you could say our passion for golf differs drastically! I was finally realizing how much my husband's golf game had improved since the previous year. I guess all the chipping and putting in the house during the winter months paid off while I sat on the sidelines (aka the couch) and watched a movie or one of my favorite TV shows.

That one sunny day swinging golf clubs, as my husband and I were enjoying the outdoors together, I hit a few not-so-good shots in a row. Then the words came to me as if they were screaming, "I told you that you are just mediocre. You are not really great at anything you do. You are only half-great." I started to play this repeatedly in my head and especially when I hit a not-so-good shot.

This activity that my husband and I love doing together instantly became a place of torture for my confidence and a prison for my identity. *That's true,* I said to myself. *I am not really great at any of the sports or activities I love. Walking and hiking. I am good at those, so I should probably stick with those.*

I began to have this dialogue in my head as I walked to the ball to hit it again: *Jess, what or who are you comparing yourself to that defines you as mediocre?* and *Jess, you haven't been really great at any sport.* I mean, what happened to just enjoying the sport and enjoying being outside? I don't know. That's when I knew I was letting something or someone else define who I was and my capabilities.

## The Truth

Deeply rooted within me, I knew it wasn't because of golf (or anything else, for that matter). It was because I didn't think I was enough. Not being able to swing my club properly to hit the ball sent a message to my brain: *See, you aren't good enough.* There was no specific person I was comparing myself to, but I knew someone out there was better than I was. Thinking that made me feel small and insignificant. We can't be thankful just because we have more than someone else. That's false humility. Our thankfulness should stem from the fact that when were born into this world we had nothing, and we can look at our lives now and be thankful for everything He has brought to fruition and blessed us with. 1 Timothy 6:6–8 reminds us this truth:

*Of course, godliness with contentment is great gain. For we brought nothing into the world, and neither can we carry anything out of it. But if we have food and clothing, we will be content with these.*

If we are only thankful when we know someone has less, then what is our response when we know someone who has more? Most of us would not respond with a thankful heart. More than likely we would respond with something like "I wish I had more like they do. I am not enough unless I have more."

When we can get to this place of thankfulness because of everything He has given us since birth, that takes our humility to a whole new level. Your thankfulness is no longer based on what someone has or doesn't have; it is rooted in Christ. Just like author Hannah Anderson says in her book *Humble Roots*, "If your thankfulness is rooted in comparison, it will evaporate in an instant." I was desperate for the truth. I was desperate to just enjoy the sport again without having this feeling every time I hit the ball not so well. So, I simply asked Him, and He responded with what so many of need to remind ourselves more often: "Jess, you are good."

A couple things about this situation. One, I was taking way too much responsibility for my abilities. I felt like I should be better because of how much we played, even though I didn't spend much time practicing. Entitlement led me to these mediocre feelings. And two, I was making this all about me: my strength. My might. My power. As you can see, I was so consumed with how good I wanted to be that I couldn't see how good I already was. (And I am not just talking about golf here.)

The Lord continued to press in. As I grumbled beneath my breath about how much golf had stolen my joy because I wasn't *the best*, He did only what He does best: He said, "Will you raise others up that are better than you? Will you do my work regardless of how good you look?" I should probably note here that my husband was hitting some amazing shots, and I failed to tell him how well he was doing—mainly because I was bitter about how not so well I was doing. Why would I have anything nice to say to him when I wasn't doing well and he was? Lord, have mercy on me! I didn't want to acknowledge how well my husband was doing because he was doing better than I was.

I believe this is why we have a hard time realizing that there is so much room in the Kingdom! I believe this is why we spend so much time comparing ourselves. We are so self-absorbed about what we are not as gifted at, that anyone who is more gifted in that area than we are immediately becomes a threat. It's as if their gifting makes us smaller. It deflates our ego and hurts our pride. Instead of saying, "Great job! You are so gifted at this," we would rather turn our heads out of jealousy, drop our heads out of self-pity, or talk about them out of comparison.

So, I looked at my husband as soon as the Lord was done pressing in and told him that he was doing a really great job that day with his short game and drives. (Double bonus for me, because words of affirmation are one of his top love languages.) Our energy shouldn't be wasted on what we are not gifted at. It should be spent encouraging others in their strengths, which we may be weak in, and asking the Lord to refine the gifts He has given to us.

*We have different gifts according to the grace given to each of us.* (Romans 12:6)

There is no comparison in Christ. The more you begin to press into Him to show you your gifts, the less you will be focused on what others have that you feel like you are missing out on. What are you good at? What brings you joy? What comes naturally to you? It's easy to disregard our gifts because we don't see them as anything but normal, when others could see them as supernatural. God is so good that He created each of us with a purpose and a design and a gift so that all of us could work together harmoniously—not so that we would constantly be at war with one another.

Paul wrote so much truth about who we are (and how good we already are) in Ephesians 1:3–14:

*Praise be to the God and Father of our Lord Jesus Christ, who has blessed us in the heavenly realms with **every spiritual blessing** in Christ. For **He chose us in him** before the creation of the world to be **holy and blameless in His sight**. In love, **He predestined us for adoption as sons** through Jesus Christ, in accordance with His pleasure and will—to the praise of His glorious grace, which He has freely given us in the One he loves. In Him **we have redemption through his blood**, the **forgiveness of sins**, in accordance with the riches of God's grace that He lavished on us. With all wisdom and understanding, **He made known to us the mystery of His will** according to His good pleasure, which He purposed in Christ, to be put into effect when the times reach their fulfillment—to bring unity to all things in heaven and on earth under Christ.*

***In Him we were also chosen**, having been **predestined according to the plan of Him** who works out everything in conformity with the purpose of His will, in order that we, who were the first to put our hope in Christ, might be for the praise of His glory. And you also were included in Christ when you heard the message of truth, the gospel of your salvation. **When you believed, you were marked in him with a seal, the promised Holy Spirit**, who is a deposit guaranteeing **our inheritance** until the redemption **of those who are God's possession**—to the praise of his glory.*

This scripture is a reminder that we are redeemed, we have an inheritance, there are promises for each of us, there are forgiveness and salvation, and we are chosen by Him and for Him. We are indeed a part of His family. This is the truth. Yet, all I could focus on was that silly golf game that slowly began to strip me of who I thought I was.

I don't know what has been robbing you or stealing your identity lately, but you need to take note. What is it? Have you thought about it lately? Or have you become so numb to what's going on in your life that you don't even know what you are thinking about? That thing that keeps stealing your identity will only continue to get worse unless you face it head-on. Where that pain comes from could be five levels deep or more, where a root of "not feeling good enough" started.

How do we begin to live this out in our lives? We must begin the process of stripping everything that steals our identity. I am not saying you will be getting rid of things for good. To heal, the cycle must stop and/or be redirected. Time doesn't heal the pain. Pain heals in time if you work on it with Him. When it comes to golf for me, I make sure to pay attention to how I am speaking to myself. More importantly, I haven't been going out with my husband as much. I may let him go practice and such while I do something else. I'm not avoiding it, but I'm working through it. I also planned golf lessons to help get me on the right track. It wasn't that He told me to give it up, but I knew He asked me to make some changes.

Maybe for you it looks like drinking more water. Maybe it looks like scheduling time when you look at your phone. Maybe He is calling you into a deep season of rest. It's not about rules of what must go or stay. Only He knows that for you and only you know His response. Your pain may be your husband. If so, I would pray and ask the Lord to reveal what pain is in your heart. Note that you aren't asking for Him to change your husband, but rather for Him to begin to change you. It always starts with us. It starts with us making the decision that we don't want to think or live this way anymore. I hated how I felt when I hit those not-so-good shots. So, I created a plan with Him on how to work through it. Now it's time for you to work on a plan with Him for how you will work through your own feelings of mediocrity and not being good enough.

That's how you begin to live a life of freedom: by giving Him the reigns and you giving up control. Not in your strength. Not in your might. Not in your power. You are going to feel lighter when you sit with those uncomfortable feelings of shame, guilt, and regret, and release them to Him.

A woman who knows she is worth more endures suffering, has joy despite any circumstances, knows that her level of thankfulness isn't based on what others have or don't have, and constantly says, "How is this happening for me, not to me?" When you received Christ, you got instant access to freedom. You are no longer a slave.

## Humility

One year at a business conference I experienced one of my first stings of what rejection felt like by someone who I had looked up to. I was in my early 20s and it was one of the first business conferences I ever attended. It was so exciting to be around people and meet people who were always showing up on my social media feeds. It was a great experience to be able to meet those who had paved the way for those who were just starting out. It was the leaders than many wanted to meet, me included.

I am not the type of person to rush up to someone I would consider a mentor, push other people out of the way to get to them, or go crazy once I meet them. Usually it's all happening within—the excitement and the wanting to ask more questions. I've been known to hover to wait my turn, but as soon as I feel the awkwardness I usually back off and let them have their space. Maybe it was insecurity that kept me from moving forward, or it could have been that I want to treat them like I would want to be treated in that situation. I would say it's probably a little bit of both.

During this business conference I was walking down a pretty

empty hallway when I spotted a leader who I considered a mentor. I told myself I was going to approach her, introduce myself, take a selfie together, and be on my way. She was talking with one other leader but didn't seem to be in a big hurry, so I made my way up to her. "Hey," I said. "My name is Jessica Vaughn and I really love all that you do for us." *Okay Jess, what are you going to say next?* I asked myself. But, as I was beginning to talk she looked at me (and she did say thanks), looked down at her phone, and then did the pull-away. (You know, when someone is talking to you, and you don't really want to talk or have time to talk, so you slowly inch away to give them the hint.) Rejection sank into the pit of my stomach, and in that moment, I regretted approaching her. This whole encounter, which lasted no more than two minutes, made me feel that, because I wasn't on top as a leader, I wasn't worth talking to—as if I was beneath her.

I obviously can't say if that is how she felt, but the insecurity within me that met with what felt like rejection and unworthiness settled deep into my heart. *What am I doing at this business conference?* I began to say to myself. *I'm not on top. I am not on the leaderboards.* Maybe she was in a hurry. Maybe she was in the middle of something. Maybe it had nothing to do with me. But it's been about five years since that conference and I can still feel the sting of rejection. It was a broken piece of myself that I didn't know at the time. Even though rejection likes to show its ugly face from time to time, the Lord has taught me and showed me to use it for good. (This is where nothing that happens to us is wasted.) It's taught me a lot about humility.

See, I never want anyone else to feel rejection like I have, so I go out of my way to try and make people feel comfortable to be open and raw with me because I could stand on the sidelines and say, "Me too." Maybe that's why I am so honest in my books: so that you could sit wherever you are reading this and say, "Me too."

Here are a few things about humility I wanted to note:
- Humility says, "I can't do this without You."
- Humility reminds us that we are grounded in the character of God.
- Humility is a heart attitude.
- Humility tells us that we our incapable of saving ourselves.
- Humility tells us that it's our sin for His righteousness.
- Humility isn't about defending yourself when falsely accused.
- Humility is about defending the truth but not on the account of our own ego or reputation.
- Humility is about us being dependent on the One and realizing we can't do anything without Him.

When we look at Google's definition of *humility*—"a modest or low view of one's own importance"—it is almost saying we should see ourselves as less important than someone else. If I didn't know Jesus and His heart, then I would think I need to lower myself to raise others up. I'm humble if I think less of myself. God is not telling us to view ourselves as less important than anyone else. He is calling us to live in humility and to value others above ourselves. Philippians 2:3–4 says:

*Do nothing out of selfish ambition or vain conceit. Rather, in humility value others above ourselves, not looking to your own interests but each of you to the interests of others.*

We are still worthy. We are still loved. But, making sure what we do in this life isn't about how it will only affect us or make us better. Vain conceit is pride. Selfish ambition is elevating one's self-interest before others. If I do what feels good to me and only what I think is right, then how will my husband feel? If I have an attitude of "Well, if they don't agree, then they don't have to stay," how does that help anyone? We see this a lot on social media. People delete friends they have been friends with for years because they disagree on a subject. You can insert your own saying that maybe you have said a time or two. It's entitlement. It's thinking we deserve more than we do. Much of it stems from pain from the past. (I know mine did.) It's why you are here, reading this book. You don't want to walk around in pain anymore. You want to understand you are worth more and so are your neighbor, your husband, your children, your family, and your friends.

He is inviting us to dine with Him as children dependent upon a Father for their daily needs and wants. Food. Shelter. Safety. And everything in between. He is not inviting you to ignore yourself, either. That's false humility.

In Matthew 18:1, we see the disciples asking Jesus about who is the greatest:

*At that time, the disciples came to Jesus, saying, "Who is the greatest in the kingdom of heaven?"*

I love that this same question applies to you and to me still today! *Am I next to be chosen, God, to be the leader? To be the one on top? Who am I greater than?* Shortly before Matthew 18, in Matthew 17, we see Jesus predict His death for a second time: *"The disciples we filled with grief"* (Matthew 17:23), yet they quickly forgot what was really coming and began to worry about their own future. Pride versus humility—which is why Jesus clearly calls us to go back to how we started, where we depended on our mother and father for everything, like our daily nourishment, where He calls us to be children again to enter the Kingdom of heaven.

*He called a little child to him, and placed the child among them. And he said: "Truly I tell you, unless you change and become like little children, you will never enter the kingdom of heaven. Therefore, whoever takes the lowly position of this child is the greatest in the kingdom of heaven. And whoever welcomes one such child in my name welcomes me.*
(Matthew 18:2–5)

We know Google's definition of humility. Now let's look at what biblical humility looks like. To sum it up, it is knowing that we have a God, whose power is endless. A God who calms the storms and causes the storms. A God who not only sits at a table of sinners but reclines back in His chair with them. (See Mark 2:15.) A God who is full of grace and mercy. The other part of this humility definition is knowing that we are human. Therefore, we are limited in our abilities and our strength. We can plan things, have goals, and have desires, but only God can bring those ideas and desires to life. Pride says, "I can do this all on my own." Humility says, "I can't do anything on my own." When we act proudly, we actually place ourselves in opposition to God, "but he gives more grace. That is why Scripture says, 'God opposes the proud, but gives grace to the humble'" (James 4:6). I also think of Matthew 23:12 quite often in this adventurous life with Jesus: *"For those who exalt themselves will be humbled, and those who humble themselves will be exalted."*

What do you really gain by being prideful? By pushing ahead instead of patiently waiting on the Lord? Temporary, fleeting feelings of seeds of success that were planted in the wrong soil and at any minute could be scorched.

A few questions to constantly ask yourself are:
- *Why do I want this?*
- *Why am I doing this?*
- *What will be gained from this?*

Apply this to your life now. Write down the desires on your heart. Then begin to ask the three questions above to make sure your heart is in alignment with His. Make sure that what you are pursuing is something you want to pursue and not just what you see others pursuing. Be aware, make your desires known, and then begin to live them out knowing you can't do any of this without Him!

## Chapter 5
# For the Love of Money

≡

It was just a normal day. I had my list of things that needed to be done, and one of them was going to the grocery store. (Grocery shopping is never my favorite thing to do. Sometimes it just overwhelms me. Thankfully I only needed to pick up a few things that day.) I usually opt for the self-checkout line, but that day I got in line to check out with a cashier. As I took out my card to pay, I noticed a woman a few lines down taking things off her total and then putting them on again. I knew she was trying to find the "right" amount so she could pay for her groceries. I swiped my card and began the process of paying for my groceries. I looked down at the screen to see what my next prompt was when God stepped in and decided to change the course of my next 15 minutes.

"Jess, I want you to pay for that woman's groceries," He said to me. Of course, my response was *Are you sure you want me to pay? God, is this really you? Are you 100% sure you want me to pay?* I can't imagine what this conversation would sound like if I said it out loud. It was full of question and uncertainty, because I knew if I paid for her groceries then this fear I had (of not having enough money) would consume me. On the other hand, I knew I was going to be able to bless someone who needed it the most in the moment. I finished paying for my groceries and thanked the cashier. Off I went to the register a few lanes down to ask the woman if I could pay for her groceries. She did what most of us would do: She fought me a little bit. "You don't have to do that. It's okay! Thank you, though," she said. After much persistence, she finally agreed to allow me to pay for her groceries. Once she agreed, she spoke a few words that I'll never forget: "Why do you want to help me or do something like this for me?" I could tell this woman just wasn't having a good day and she was a woman who seemed to be filled with bitterness. She was an older woman, and you could tell she was a matter-of-fact kind of woman. I wish I could tell you that I had some witty or great Jesus-loving response, but I didn't. My response was "Just because I want to buy your groceries." The cashier double-checked with me to make sure it was okay to proceed. I confirmed, and she began to pull more things out from behind the counter that I didn't see or know I would be paying for. After paying for her groceries, I helped the woman get her things to the car. The next day the Lord revealed Hebrews 13:2 to me: *"Do not forget to show hospitality to strangers, for by so doing some people have shown hospitality to angels without knowing it."*

The Lord was teaching me a lesson about obedience and kindness, but most importantly He was trying to help me realize how much money controlled my emotions. It's not that

I didn't want to help this woman. It was that money meant something to me, and I was determined to figure it out. Well, really it was more like the Lord was determined to show me.

## Remembering Where it Began

The theme throughout my life has always been that I would never be good enough. It's what I felt when I went through a break-up, when my parents fought, when I was being gossiped about in high school, when I was told I was too short, and the list goes on. Every time something happened I internalized it as me not being good enough. I never tried to be enough. I just sunk deeper and deeper into the fact I would never be what someone wants me to be and I would never be someone who changes the world. I would just be someone who misses the mark because of the way I grew up and because of the things that I have done or that have happened to me.

"You are not good enough" is what I heard when things were said to me like "You just wait 'til you get older and have to pay bills. Then you'll see" and "You are not going to have enough money to do that." *When will someone believe in me? When will someone tell me I am enough? Not more than enough or not good enough, but just enough?*

Growing up, I had to give money for gas whenever I wanted and needed to go somewhere. I felt like every time I needed anything, I had to give money first, whether it was a ride to my friend's house or a ride to work. If I didn't give money, it led to a big fight about how I didn't care about what was being done for me. I heard repeatedly that I didn't appreciate anything if the exchange of money wasn't involved. I heard as a child how much money other people had or how a certain person could do this or that because their husband made a certain amount of money. Comparison was almost always involved when it came to money in our house.

Money was a negative topic. It was like a cuss word. It wasn't about abundance, and it wasn't about a blessing. It was more about how there was never enough and there would never be enough no matter what I did, how hard I tried, or how many jobs I had. I was taught that money was equivalent to how much I loved someone else. If pennies were stolen from my piggy bank and I asked why, I was questioned about my love for that person—even though I wasn't asked about anyone borrowing the money. I was questioned about whether I really cared about the other person.

Three strong lies about money were engrained into my head at a very early age. One, you must work hard for your money, and even when you do work hard for your money there will never be enough. You better work, because no one else will take care of you. Two, how much money you have equals how successful you are. Three, money equals love.

Can we agree that those three things can be a recipe for disaster? The thing is, when you are younger you don't know how you form those beliefs. Then, as you get older those beliefs begin to mature and take control in your life. Your actions become what you believe about money. The way you live is formed by those beliefs. How you treat others stems from those beliefs.

It typically looks something like entitlement, self-righteousness, being a victim, anger, and bitterness. The way I lived in my teens and throughout my 20s was all about entitlement, and what I thought I deserved or what I thought people owed me because of what had been done to me. I was self-righteous because I was the one who took care of me, and I thought I didn't need help (or anyone else, for that matter). Since I was able to survive in my teens doing it myself without help, then I surely wouldn't need it going into my adult years. I felt like a victim because every time something happened to me I would think, *Why me?* I had anger because of my childhood and bitterness because I got to witness other people get what I could only dream about at the time.

Then I had a huge wake-up call. When was I going to stop blaming my past for who I was in the present? I am old enough to know right and wrong. I am old enough to learn how to budget money, steward money, and create my own beliefs surrounding money. But, I could never live in the present because I blamed so much of my past for where I was. We must get to a point where the past is no longer to blame. We must get to a point where we say, "This is enough," and start taking responsibility for our thoughts and actions.

## The Words that Changed the Course of My Life

When I first met my husband, my life was comfortable. (At

the time, I didn't realize how comfortable I was.) I was working hard and putting in the hours. I knew how to hustle and I knew how to work. I had my savings built up, I was independent, and I didn't need anyone else's help financially. I could take care of myself. (That's all my pride and ego talking.) Little did I know that the way I was living and everything I thought I knew about myself were about to be completely wrecked shortly after meeting my husband.

One day I was on the phone with my spiritual dad at the time, PJ McClure. He spoke words to me that forever changed the course of my life. PJ said, "Jess, if you worry that much about money"—I gulped and he continued—"then maybe God should take it all away and see how you feel then." *No. No, thank you. I would rather not experience that. I am happy here. I feel safe here. I know what I am doing here.* Little did PJ know, the words he spoke to me that day would be a prophesy that would begin to unfold.

At the time, my husband was experiencing a completely God-led season in his business. Although he was putting in all the hours necessary, the income wasn't matching his work. Therefore, I stepped in and helped when needed. I wish I could say I helped with a gracious heart, but I was so bitter to see the Lord, in fact, begin to take it all away. Jon and I were engaged at the time and well on our way to being married, and this was one of my first lessons the Lord was going to be teaching me when it came to money and marriage. I say this was a God-led season because He was teaching both my soon-to-be husband and me how to communicate about money, how to trust and rely on Him, and how to choose each other (our marriage) over money. I was determined to not let the enemy steal my marriage before it even began.

It was one of those seasons in which you feel like everything that is happening is an expense. Here are a few examples: The ceiling in our townhouse flooded and fell through. It contained mold, to which I had a severe allergic reaction. A rock flew into my windshield and cracked it. The same thing happened to my husband. My website crashed, and many things weren't working on it. Many things, big and small, were happening in addition to these examples. I know this is life and things do happen, but this wasn't the right season for me for things to just happen. It felt like I was losing control, and I only became angrier and feared more.

What I feared the most as the money began to slowly go away was that I would be forced to live the way I had to growing up. It scared me into an obsession about money. I didn't want to ever experience those feelings again. This made me also realize how much my life revolved around how much money I had. However much I had made me feel safe and reminded me that I wasn't going to have to live that way again. When I realized that soon it could all be taken away, everything I did from that point on was out of fear. I worked out of fear, for example. I hustled to make money, out of fear; I didn't work out of joy or wanting to help people. My work became dollar signs; I kept telling myself, "You can't go back there." It's when we become completely stripped of our obsession—the thing we are a slave to, or worry about the most—that we realize how much of our life was defined by it. It wasn't until the Lord slowly took it away that I was able to see how much of what I did stemmed from fear. If I didn't work, then I felt guilty because I wasn't producing. If I rested then I began to tell myself, *You are lazy and you should be more productive.*

Brace yourself for what I am about to share with you. Throughout that year and half that my husband and I endured together one truth remained: Whether I had money or didn't have money, I still worried about money. Therefore, money wasn't the issue. My heart toward money was the issue.

## The Heart Issue

So often we think that having more money would solve all our problems. One thing is for sure: You can't buy your way to happiness. You can buy your way to temporary, fleeting happiness. But you cannot buy your way (or save your way) to eternal happiness. If I had more money, then I would buy even healthier foods, and then I would love myself. If I had more money, I could pay off this credit card debt, and then I would be happy. If we made more money, then my husband and I wouldn't fight as much. It's easy to think that having more equals more happiness. What about the people who do have all the money and end up divorced and miserable? What about those who can afford all the fancy equipment and trainers but still hate themselves or are miserable? This is what I mean when I say you can't buy happiness.

Yes, I understand money is needed for food, clothing, and shelter. I also understand that your wanting more money could help any one of those areas. I 100% understand. I also understand that our need for Jesus needs to be more than any of those needs. It's tough and it's work, but His way is simple, not easy. It's easy to form Jesus into who we want Him to be and when He doesn't pull through the way we wanted Him to, then we form Him into someone who doesn't care at all. When do we get to a point where we say, "He is worth it. No matter what it costs me right now—friends, family, work, or ranks—He is worth it."?

Friend, I am with you. I am on the same side, in the trenches, asking Him the same questions as you. *Lord, show me how! Lord, teach me how! Lord, I want to abandon it all, but in my power, I don't know how.*

In Matthew 19:16–22 we encounter a man who wants to follow Jesus and have eternal life:

*Now behold, one came and said to Him, "Good Teacher, what good thing shall I do that I may have eternal life?"*

*So, He said to him, "Why do you call Me good? No one is good but One, that is, God. But if you want to enter into life, keep the commandments."*

*He said to Him, "Which ones?"*

*Jesus said, "'You shall not murder,' 'You shall not commit adultery,' 'You shall not steal,' 'You shall not bear false witness,' 'Hon-*

*or your father and your* mother,' *and, 'You shall love your neighbor as yourself.'"*

*The young man said to Him, "All these things I have kept from my youth. What do I still lack?"*

*Jesus said to him, "If you want to be perfect, go, sell what you have and give to the poor, and you will have treasure in heaven; and come, follow Me."*

*But when the young man heard that saying, he went away sorrowful, for he had great possessions.*

So, is God calling me to sell everything I have to follow Him? Is having nothing the only way to truly follow Him and have eternal life? Jesus isn't about the masses. We can see that, as He only travels with 12 disciples during His ministry before the cross. He often gave speeches or spoke in parables that rubbed people the wrong way. That turned people away. That challenged many to look inside themselves and to do the deep work. Although He may not be calling you to literally sell everything you own and live on the streets or spend your life in Africa spreading the Gospel, He does call us to sell everything in the sense of giving it all up and over to Him. Nothing comes before Him. Preaching the gospel will involve friends leaving, family disowning you, and coworkers who think you are crazy. Is He worth it?

When you give control over to Him, you actually find yourself and freedom you never realized you had. Now, this doesn't mean that we don't work. This is not about sitting back and waiting for God to bless us. We still must work because He has given us all a mission. But it's a different kind of work. It's saying, "I am going to do what I am called to today and I will let God be God." It's not working because God is on our time clock, as if He is working for us. (Don't we do that a lot? We tell God what to do or what we would like Him to do instead of asking Him what He would like for us to do.) It's different because we can show up to our workout not ready to kill ourselves so the scale will move, but because you get to move and you are going to let God be God. It's different because you are not going to try to control your husband, but you will let God be God to your husband, rather than you trying to be God to your husband.

In this situation, I felt like that rich ruler. I was holding on so tightly to money that whenever anything happened, I felt sorrow because I worked so hard for it. I believe that we often take a scripture that makes us uncomfortable and challenges us to make it fit our needs and say that we cannot relate to it or that it does not apply to us. For example: I don't have a lot of money, so I can't relate to this rich ruler. Oh, yes, you can relate to this rich ruler. You may not have a lot of money, but something else is your prized possession that you can't seem to let go of. His word is alive and well, my friend.

I knew this journey to unwrapping why I had such a tight hold on money was going to require a lot of prayer, seeking, and awareness on my part. That's how I really began to work through this season with my husband. God needed to take it away for me to gain the freedom and perspective that I didn't have before. I was so comfortable where I was before getting married, and He knew exactly what I needed. It wasn't what I *wanted*. It was what I *needed*.

Let's look at each element individually.

**Prayer**
These prayers were extremely specific. They were more cries than prayers. I was desperate to know Him more and I was desperate for Him to take this stronghold in my life away from me. I hated the way I reacted about money. I hated who I was when Jon, my husband, wanted to discuss money. I was a bitter toward my husband many times. And, many times I had to go to Jon and ask for forgiveness for the way I reacted. Let your prayers about money be specific.

Break generational curses and strongholds for your family and the generation to come. Break the spirit of poverty. Break the chains the of worry. Take how much money you have out of the equation. God isn't concerned with the dollar amount. He's good for it. Go to Him in prayer as if you have nothing. Nada. Be with Him. Spend time with Him. Let your prayers be bold. You—yes, you!—can be the one who changes the course of your family's history. It doesn't have to be "This is the way it has always been and this is the way it always will be." Stand. Rise. Declare new territory over your finances and call on Him. I remember constantly saying to myself while I paid bills, "Money does not define me. Money, you have no control over me." That's like a sword cutting right into the plan of the enemy.

*Seek God while he's here to be found, pray to him while he's close at hand. Let the wicked abandon their way of life and the evil their way of thinking. Let them come back to* GOD, *who is merciful, come back to our God, who is lavish with forgiveness.* (Isaiah 55:6–7)

## Seeking

I spent so much time seeking answers. I wanted to know where all of us this came from to begin with and just how long it had been going on. I asked Him to show me. When specific situations arose, I sought to get to the root of it. (A lot of the times this caused much repentance.) It was a constant pursuit to think less about money and more about Him. (If I am being honest and totally transparent, He is still working on me in this area. Like author and speaker Alisa Keeton said in a Revelation Wellness training, "If it's not good, then it's not the end.")

## Awareness

By now you should be aware of the problem. We typically go through phases of revelation with the Lord as He begins to peel back different layers at different times, according to when He thinks we are ready. Sometimes we just need Him to rip off the bandage and let the wound bleed so that we can properly heal over time instead of receiving just a temporary fix.

It started with prayer, it continued with seeking, and it ends with awareness for my everyday life. Whether I am at the grocery store, as in the story I shared earlier in the chapter, or at a drive-through window, it's the willingness to invite the Holy Spirit into every mundane task to show us just exactly where our thoughts lead. *Lord, make me aware of my choices. Lord, help me be aware when I am choosing money over someone or something else.* It doesn't have to be perfect. It's an invitation. Let's throw out this need for perfection and that it must only be in a quiet space with no one around. Let's throw out all the lies that we aren't spiritual enough or don't have this or that. When you have awareness, it changes everything. It no longer allows the bandage to be reapplied. It allows you to continue to work on the root issue itself. Awareness is tough, and you won't always get it right. Have grace and know this: If it's not good, then it's not the end.

\*\*\*

Coming out of this season, my husband and I took a step of faith as he left his job of six years and had built himself. It wasn't an easy step of faith, but we knew what we were doing wasn't working, and we also knew God was transitioning us into something better. He brought my husband a new job after he didn't work for a few months. During that season I felt like everything landed on me to provide for our family, and the worry and fear stole so much joy out of my business and my life. I got burned out more than I ever had before. So, is the suffering worth the lesson? Is the suffering worth the pain and the discomfort? Yes. Even though I fought with God all the way through it, I am more aware than ever today about my reactions toward money. If I didn't experience what I experienced, then I would still be comfortable harboring my feelings, and living and working out of fear.

I have said that I don't want this book to be something you read and then put it away, only to not remember. I want this book to be an experience that not only makes you say, "Me too," but one in which you put the book down and do the work. Friend, *you are worth more*. It has taken me time to realize that I must believe I was worth His sacrifice. It takes prayer. It takes seeking. It takes awareness. But, we can't do any of those three things without first experiencing the suffering that gets us to notice a piece or part of our life that isn't aligned with His will. 1 Peter 2:21 reminds us: *"For God called you to do good, even if it means suffering, just as Christ suffered for you. He is your example, and you must follow in His steps."*

Here's the good news: *"After you have suffered for a little while, the God of all grace, who called you to His eternal glory in Christ, will Himself perfect, confirm, strengthen, and establish you"* (1 Peter 5:10).

## Chapter 6
## New Wineskin

≡

It was at the end of my workout, my eyes were closed, and I was laying on my mat, when I clearly heard the Lord tell me, "Why do you keep trying to live in your old body? Do you want me to remind you how unhappy you were? Live now. Live in your new body."

I haven't been the same since.

You can read a lot about my journey with my body image in my first book, *Know Your Worth*, but just in case you haven't read it, let me share what my journey has looked like over the years.

Fitness started out as a tool—something that would bring me joy. I felt like it was something I could, for the first time, sustain (and control) in my life. At about the same time that I began my fitness journey, I became a fitness coach and business owner. That instantly put me around a bunch of other people who also wanted the best for themselves and using fitness as a tool.

What was once a tool—an outlet—for me, quickly became my obsession. So much of my time, my thoughts, and my life were surrounded by workouts, helping others with their workouts, and what food to eat. That was my life: food and workouts. Food was no longer about eating to sustain, it was about what foods would make me look just right. Even as far back as high school, during my junior and senior years, I watched what I ate and thought that 100-calorie packs were the way to go.

Life began to pass me by. I spent five years of my life chasing perfection with exhaustion around every corner. For the last two, I have been on the train to freedom. In 2014, when I wrote *Know Your Worth*, I really began to discover just how much of my life was consumed with how I looked.

Bringing you to the present day, I am writing this book in late 2017. I continue to realize how much of my time was spent trying to get something back—trying to get my old body back but with a new mind.

## The Journey

From year five to year seven, I started to decrease my workouts and my time in the gym, and I slowly began to cut back how much I posted about it. I started to unfollow people who triggered me to want to be perfect. I unfollowed people who I allowed to make me feel less than and as though I didn't do enough to get the body I so often craved (key words: *I allowed*). Although I began to move slower in certain areas of my life, the enemy was always around the corner with new tactics to try and steal my joy. Then came thoughts of *If I don't work out as much, then I won't look as pretty. If I don't work out as much, then I won't look the way I used to. If I don't work out as much, then I will only begin to gain weight.* All lies. No truth. So, as I was trying to cut back and work on this, new thoughts about my new routine began to haunt me just as much.

Then everything about fitness and health changed for me in one day. I was in the doctor's office for my annual checkup. As she was feeling around my throat, she addressed her concern about how swollen it felt. I made an appointment for an ultrasound. Praise God, my nodes were not cancerous, but I knew this was a new journey. Bloodwork revealed the reasons why I had been so tired and so exhausted (especially after my workouts). Of course, in these types of situations, panic begins to set in, and you begin to wonder how you will be able to change things and what you can do. This proved to me that the way I was "doing" life wasn't going to sustain me for much longer. Seven years of hustle in business and in my fitness had begun to slowly shut down my body. I wasn't just tired mentally and spiritually. My body was saying, "Me too." The explanation that my doctor gave me was that I was running 100 miles per hour, while by body was on E. Every day I would wake up and go-go-go without any gas in the tank. We all know what happens when a car continues to run on no gas: It stalls and then comes to a complete stop—with the possibility of messing other things up.

This meant less-intense workouts. This meant cleaning up

some things regarding what I ate. This meant more walks than sprint intervals. It was a change of pace I had never experienced before. It was slower. And, it was exactly where God wanted me to be.

When the Lord spoke to me that day I knew that, although my heart received Jesus and I love Him with all that I have, I wasn't fully accepting the price He paid on the cross for me. I opened my journal and began to write. Those words that the Lord spoke brought everything that I was feeling into light. He brought it to my attention. He wanted me to understand—not to torture me, but to remind me of His love. I had been working on my freedom, trying to figure out why I couldn't let this go. *Why is the way my body looks so important to me? Why do I feel upset sometimes when I look in the mirror and don't see the muscles and definition I once had? Am I ready for this?* I was *working* for my freedom instead of *receiving* my freedom. He was bringing my pain to light. He was bringing my striving to light. He was bringing whatever was buried to surface.

As I began to write, Mark 2:21–22 began to play over and over in my head:

*No one sews a patch of unshrunk cloth to an old garment. Otherwise, the new piece will pull away from the old, making the tear worse. And no one pours new wine into old wineskins. Otherwise, the wine will burst the skins, and both the wine and the wineskins will be ruined. No, they pour* **new wine** *into* **new wineskins***.*

*Okay, Lord, you have my attention!* There I was, trying to sew a good, healthy patch to an old body that was worn out. Maybe you are mom who is still living in an old wineskin because you want the body you had before you had your child(ren). You are working so hard to get something back when He is calling you to the new wineskin, which is now—your new body. Maybe you are a single woman trying to get back your former body, because you felt like you received the most attention when you looked that way.

Our old bodies died in baptism and rose anew with Him. We begin to believe the lie that what we used to have was better than what we have now. As the Lord said to me, I say to you: Would you like me to remind you how you felt in that old body? That old wineskin? Not how you looked or appeared, but how you *felt*. When I think about how I felt in my old wineskin, feelings of low self-esteem come up. Feelings that say *You need to do more and work harder.* Joy wasn't found in the old, so why did I want the old? Let me repeat the same questions back to you: Were you really happy in the old? Why are you wanting the old back? Get real with yourself. No fluff.

I do bet that you will find the same feelings in the old as you are trying to live in the new. I know I did. That's where we must realize that joy isn't in the old or the new, it's in who He is. The One who sustains. You could have the perfect body tomorrow, but I guarantee that the joy would be fleeting because it isn't built on a firm foundation. Something in your life could rob you of that joy and remind you that you aren't beautiful or worthy. You have the perfect body you have always wanted but feel like you aren't worthy. I have seen it time and time again when people lose weight and get to where they want to be, but they look in the mirror and still see the overweight person staring back at them. They see the old wineskin, not new. I hope you are beginning to realize that this has nothing to do with health and fitness.

You would think that after the word the Lord gave me that things would begin to ease up a bit. I was wrong—really wrong. It was only the beginning. As we continue this journey, I want to remind you of what Paul wrote in 2 Corinthians 5:1–10:

*For we know that when this earthly tent we live in is taken down (that is, when we die and leave this earthly body), we will have a house in heaven, an eternal body made for us by God himself and not by human hands. We grow weary in our present bodies, and we long to put on our heavenly bodies like new clothing. For we will put on heavenly bodies; we will not be spirits without bodies. While we live in these earthly bodies, we groan and sigh, but it's not that we want to die and get rid of these bodies that clothe us. Rather, we want to put on our new bodies so that these dying bodies will be swallowed up by life. God himself has prepared us for this, and as a guarantee he has given us his Holy Spirit.*

*So, we are always confident, even though we know that if we live in these bodies we are not at home with the Lord. For we live by believing and not by seeing. Yes, we are fully confident, and we would rather be away from these earthly bodies, for then we will be at home with the Lord. So, whether we are here in this body or away from this body, our goal is to please him. For we must all stand before Christ to be judged. We will each receive whatever we deserve for the good or evil we have done in this earthly body.*

As I began to dive deeper into my health situation in February 2017 and the road to recovery, I realized that beyond me just trying to live in old wineskin, I was also carrying so much "weight" in my body that I could not seem to get rid of. One of the biggest issues with my health was my digestion. My food was just sitting in my stomach and wasn't breaking down, which in turn was making me irritable and tired. I had days when I wanted to break down and cry because of how miserable it felt. My focus for so long had been how was my body going to look. Now, I didn't care about how it looked; I just wanted to feel better. I wanted to have energy again. I wanted to be in a better mood and not snap at my husband. Everything I wanted had to do with how I felt, not how I looked. It was a longing for my body to feel whole.

I was angry and I was frustrated. People noted that I didn't look the way I used to and I heard, "You are skinny. I can't believe something is wrong." I am sure they meant well, but it went right to my heart. I was angry about what was happening to me. I felt like this was my punishment for past sins. I was frustrated by how long it was taking to heal. Patience? I didn't have it. Can you relate? With an angry and frustrated heart, I pulled out my journal again and began the journey to healing not just my body, but all of me.

*Heal me, Lord, and I will be haled; save me and I will be saved, for you are the one I praise.*
(Jeremiah 17:14)

## Forgiveness

What began as my body beginning to shut down as it was running on E quickly became a place where the Lord was teaching me. It was as if this was His way of getting my attention, to slow me down and to show me what was really going on with me and inside of me. My heart began to go from frustrated and angry to *Lord, how is this helping me for my future?* Constantly on repeat is *Lord, what are you teaching me here? How can I experience more of you?* Yes, in my pain. Yes, in those moments when I want to break down out of confusion as to why, I can ask Him how to bring Him glory. That is where we begin to go from victim to victor. The same Father who said, *"This is my Son, whom I love; with Him I am well pleased"* in Matthew 3:17 is the same Father who by His *"Spirit led Jesus, His son, into the wilderness to be tempted by the devil"* (see Matthew 4:1–11). Come on now! The same Father said, "I love you so much. Now go be tempted."

This reminds me that every trial we face isn't just the enemy coming against us. It's an opportunity for the us to ask the Lord, "What are you trying to teach me?" Read through the Book of Jonah. You will see the Lord appoints the whale, the storm, and the scorching heat as well. The Lord can appoint things to get our attention to get us back on track for His will for our lives. We have to be brave enough and bold enough to say, "I'm listening, Lord. I am here." Psalms 147:3 reminds us that *"He heals the brokenhearted and binds up their wounds."* Let's also not forget Psalm 34:18: *"The Lord is close to the brokenhearted and saves those who are crushed in spirit."* Although He may appoint things (or not) He is still close to us. He promises to stay. He promises to never leave. My friend, it is us who block the flow of His love. Through our anger, resentment, jealousy, unforgiveness, and broken hearts, we begin to place what has happened to us on God. Therefore, we think He doesn't love us, He doesn't care about us, He isn't good, and so on. Our earthly experience begins to distort the truth about the heart of the Father.

This leads me to sharing what the Lord is really working on my heart. He reminded me quickly how I stopped believing for things to happen, and I just started to try to make things happen. I asked Him during my writing exercise one morning in my journal, *Why am I experiencing this? Why do I have these certain feelings and what feels like a heavy cloud over me and this extra "weight" I can't seem to get rid of?* A simple, kind, and loving response was exactly what I needed. What He gave me was, in fact, what I needed but it was a tough and tender response. He said, "You haven't forgiven yourself." I couldn't believe that was the answer. I knew it was something I never really sat with—meaning, sitting with my own feelings about how I haven't forgiven myself for my past mistakes and sins. I have spent so much time trying to heal what has happened to me that I haven't spent enough time on me. If we don't work on ourselves first, with Him, then it is so hard for anything else to fall into place. It's building upon the wrong foundation.

Have you forgiven yourself? Have you forgiven yourself for those things you couldn't control yet blamed yourself for? More than anything, I don't want you to read this book and put it down without doing any work in between. I wouldn't be here with you if I didn't make time for the deep work myself. Put down this book. Write. Pray. Ask Him to show you what the extra "weight" you are carrying around looks like or is. We must begin to get comfortable being uncomfortable. Cry. Repent. Forgive. Fight for the truth when the lies resurface. The Lord keeps telling me He wants His people back. That's you. That's me. He wants our hearts back to where we want Him more than we want food, our children, our spouse, our family, and our friends.

So, although my body was running on E, He began to slowly peel back the layers so that I could begin to refuel with the Living Water. Forgiveness of myself was the first step.

## The Freedom Train

"You were made for this," the Lord repeated on the second day at Rev on the Road, a two-day event put on by Alisa Keeton (her ministry is Revelation Wellness) and her team of leaders. Since working through different health issues, my mind and body and soul have been craving more freedom. I could feel the heaviness I have been carrying for long. When I asked the Lord why I couldn't forgive myself, He told me it was because I have become so used to carrying the pain myself. (I am sure this is where you can raise your hand and say, "Yes. Me too.") We carry the pain around us almost like it's our punishment for the choices and decisions we have made. When we talk to people, our pain shows by how we react and respond. Our pain can also show when we don't do or say anything at all.

He reminded me that I am free, that I have always been free, but that I need to believe and receive that I am free. Do you see the pattern throughout my life? It's not receiving what Jesus did on the cross for me. I believe He did it. But, I don't believe I am worth the sacrifice. The Lord said, "Jess, you know pain. You have felt pain. Now it's time to believe you are worth the sacrifice." Over and over these words repeat, at different times in my life and different seasons of my life.

The vision the Lord me showed about worry was us being chained at the ankle to a small tree in the ground. We know we are strong enough to pull the tree down. We know we can simply take off the chain. Yet, it gets comfortable with the chain on. It gets scary to take off the chain of worry, because then we step into a place of unfamiliarity. That place is faith. It's a place where we don't try to take control or pick up control.

I love what author and speaker Alisa Keeton said to us at Rev on the Road that weekend: "We cannot change what we do not recognize." Amen! How do we forgive if we don't know that's the reason we feel so weighed down? How do we receive His sacrifice if we don't realize that believing we are worth it is the issue? I think, if I am being honest, it's just too hard. It's hard work to do the deep work. What's easy? Pointing the finger. We point the finger at God and become angry. We get mad at our children for not doing what we say. We snap at our husband because he didn't read our mind. In reality, a lot of why we do what we do usually stems from the pain—our pain, from the past that have never been dealt with or felt.

So how do we do that? We sit. We slow down. We ask the Lord to show us what's happening inside of us. Begin to allow yourself to feel whatever comes up. Anger. Bitterness. Maybe you start crying. Maybe you fall on your knees in prayer and repentance. That's exactly where He led me: into repentance of my past sexual sins. Although He had forgiven me, I needed to forgive myself.

Declare it. Speak it into repentance. Put it to death. You must make time for this work. If you don't know how to work through it by yourself, then seek help. Ask a close friend to sit with you and talk with you. Ask your husband to sit and listen to you. There are bravery, courage, and faith in asking, but also in listening to the response to help.

I am still on the freedom train with healing my body, but I am already free because of the sacrifice He made for me. You are free because of the sacrifice He made for you. Move in freedom today. Not because you *must* move but because you *get to* move. It's time to stop putting so many rules on food and workouts and get back to the joy you once had in them. I want to share three tips with you to help you overcome any destructive thoughts you may be facing right now or when they begin to surface again.

**1. Identify your triggers.** What is making you go toward those destructive thoughts? As I mentioned earlier, I spent a lot of time unfollowing people on social media and just cleaning up my social media accounts period. Health is a huge part of our life, but it shouldn't be the one thing we give all our attention to, to the point of obsession. Maybe social media isn't a trigger for you; spend time asking the Lord to reveal what your triggers are. This will take some digging deep, I know. If a person is a trigger because of what they say to you, have an open discussion with them. Even though to them it may not seem like anything, we don't know what we don't recognize, right? Then begin to set boundaries that are healthy for yourself and the other person. Boundaries are important in all kinds of relationships. I have also confessed to some people how much I compared my life to theirs. It wasn't necessarily anything they did to me, but I knew I had to repent of my thoughts and apologize for my own behavior that may have made them upset or uncomfortable out of my own need to compare. My friend, you are free. Taking steps like this is scary but the weight comes up when you don't try to harbor everything yourself.

**2. Study scripture and pray over your body.** I know this is a given. But it so overlooked sometimes. When our thoughts begin to run wild, and in the moments of self-doubt and weakness, it's so easy to look to others or numb out on social media, which can make it worse. Our goal should be to turn to Jesus in times of heartbreak, of confusion, and when you feel like the ugliest, most worthless person on this earth. It's hard, I know, especially when so many things are telling us to look a different way and do it a different way. Don't let the difficulty become an excuse. Psalm 139 started my journey to knowing my worth. It has been the foundation for my ministry. He will provide you with what you need when you go to His word. It is alive today. He will speak to you. Turn to Him.

Here are a few examples of scripture you can pray over your body. Use intention with your prayer and be bold about what you are asking for. *"Without doubt,"* as James 1:6 says.

Start off with a prayer specifically geared toward what is going on in your body. Address any pain, weakness, struggles, and idols. Address addictions and places on your body where your image is distorted, and be sure to talk about where you are on your journey with the scale and counting calories. Be as specific as possible. Place your hand on specific body parts that you begin to pray on. Then we will use scripture to pray with His truth and His word. For example: Whatever I eat or drink I will bring glory to you. No obsession or stronghold is formed, and chains are broken. Generations of disease. Broken. (See 1 Corinthians 10:31.)

*Lord, I offer up my body as a sacrifice and as a place of worship.* (See Romans 12:1–2.)

When I train my body it isn't so I can look a certain way. It's awareness that godliness has much more value than physical training. Training my mind and my body to worship and not to worry. (See 1 Timothy 4:8.)

*For you created my inmost being; you knit me together in my mother's womb. I praise you because I am fearfully and wonderfully made; your works are wonderful, I know that full well.* **My frame was not hidden from you when I was made in the secret place, when I was woven together in the depths of the earth.**

*Your eyes saw my unformed body; all the days ordained for me were written in your book before one of them came to be.*
(Psalm 139:13–16)

Your body is known to Him. It wasn't a mistake!

**3. Go back to what made you become self-destructive.** Don't run away from this one. Can you remember when you first started to have thoughts about your body and the way you looked? Do you remember where you were and what was happening? How many times since has that same pattern begun to repeat in your life? It has taken a lot of work for me to realize why I think the way I do. I wouldn't continue to talk to you about doing the deep work if I didn't know your life would change when you did. This is so crucial when it comes to your healing process. This is going to help get to the root of the problem, instead of constantly covering it up! You don't have to be a victim anymore. Those days are done. You know you are worth the work.

These three steps will take time. Give yourself grace to explore them, too. It's more than just wanting it to happen. It is willing it to happen. You are not going to want to do the deep work. But, you can will it to happen. It's going to cause you to slow down, to not move as fast. To be honest, it's going to reveal to you just how much your own strength doesn't save you or cause things to go into motion.

*Lord, we can't do this without you. Your love isn't based the shape of our bodies. Your love isn't based on the number on the scale.*

*Your love isn't based on the size of our bodies. Continue to show us what your love is based on. Which is the joy and happiness that You get from us by being alive and watching us live out Your will. Lord, let us be women who chase you and not food. Let us be women who receive your love by laying down our work, and picking up your yoke. In Jesus name, amen!*

## Chapter 7
## The Heart of the Father

≡

*I don't need to be afraid,* I kept telling myself every time I would lie down and didn't feel quite right. Jess, you don't need to be afraid. He's a good Father. *I don't need to be afraid. I don't need to be afraid.* I quoted those words (and still do) ever since I had my first episode of benign positional vertigo in February 2017. At 7:00 in the morning I shot straight up out of bed with my eyes moving from side to side so fast. The world was literally spinning, and I didn't have a clue what was happening. All of this happened within 30 seconds, but it felt like forever. Slowly my eyes came to a halt and returned to normal. My husband was beside me, and I didn't know if I should wake him up or if this was just a one-time thing. I told myself everything was okay and I began to lie back down. The world went back into a spinning frenzy, and I woke my husband up, telling him, in a panic, what was happening. After going to the doctor and realizing what it was, I felt relief, because I had an answer to what happening. What I didn't have was an answer to what was causing it.

If you have never had benign positional vertigo, it is the result of a disturbance inside your inner ear. Fluid inside tubes in your ear called semicircular canals moves when your position changes. It develops when small crystals of calcium carbonate that are normally in another area of the ear break free and find their way to the semicircular canal in your inner ear. This causes your brain to receive confusing messages about your body's position.

After spending a few days doing the half-somersault technique that was recommended, I was finally able to get relief and things seemed back to normal (except for my fear of it coming back, that is). Every night after that I would lie down and not feel right, so fear consumed me. I was afraid to move certain ways or too fast. Then, a few months later, another episode came (not as strong), which only instilled more fear into me. Maybe this was a little bit of a "The more your focus on something, the more likely it will occur or happen" type of situation. Do you do this? Something happens in your life, and then worry begins to control all your actions. The very thing you thought so much about comes to fruition and you say, "See? I told you so." I do believe that where we focus our body goes and what we think about our actions follow. It's why, in scripture, there is a constant reminding of what our thoughts should be consumed with and what our focus should be on.

*Finally, brothers and sisters, whatever is true, whatever is noble, whatever is right, whatever is pure, whatever is lovely, whatever is admirable—if anything is excellent or praiseworthy think about such things.*
(Philippians 4:8)

*What goes into someone's mouth does not defile them, but what comes out of their mouth, that is what defiles them.*
(Matthew 15:11)

*Set your minds on things above, not on earthly things. For you died, and your life is nor hidden with Christ in God. When Christ, who is your life, appears, then you also will appear with Him in glory. Put to death, therefore, whatever belongs to your earthly nature: sexual immorality, impurity, lust, evil desires, and greed, which is idolatry.*
(Colossians 3:2–5)

There was list of things I wanted to be angry with God about. Not only was it my finances in the first year of marriage with my husband and my health, but now experiencing a new level with my health that involved vertigo. In all honesty, it was my flesh throwing a pity party. The "Why me?" pity party. The party where you are the only person that shows up.

Lessons often come disguised in a mess. That's when the journey began to understand (and discover) the heart of the Father, on a much deeper level than I have before. He gives us specific instructions in His word that can sometimes seem so cut-throat.

*He calls us to abide (remain) in Him and He will remain in us.*
(John 15:4)

In working with so many women over the course of almost eight years, at the time of writing this book, I have witnessed the fear of the Lord get misinterpreted, which is why I believe many of us punish ourselves and put ourselves through our own prison: because we think that's who He is as a Father. That what you have done is no longer redeemable. That you are not worth saving. But, if we understand the heart of who He is, our perspective changes. Fearing the Lord does not mean to fear Him and who He is. It's an invitation to take refuge in Him. In our biggest messes is when we should fear Him the most. We should fear not being close with Him, not being in His presence.

We see in the Old Testament what would happen if we don't fear the Lord, and it shares what blessings will come if we do fear the Lord. Blessed is the one who fears the Lord. Fearing the Lord is corresponding with humbleness.

*I will bless those who have humble and contrite hearts, who tremble at my word.*
(Isaiah 66:2)

Pastor and author John Piper shared on his blog in a post titled "Trading Fear for Fear":

> The fear of the Lord is the fear of straying from him. Therefore, it expresses itself in taking refuge in God. That's why *two* conditions are mentioned in Psalm 31:19, "How great is the goodness you have stored up for those who fear you. You lavish it on those who come to you for protection (refuge), blessing them before the watching world." They seem to be opposites. *Fear* seems to drive away and *taking refuge* seems to draw in. But when we see that this fear is a fear of not being drawn in, then they work together.

There is a real trembling for the saints. "Work out your salvation with fear and trembling" (Philippians 2:12.) But it is the trembling one feels in the arms of a Father who has just plucked His child from the undertow of the ocean.

## Is He Good?

I believe we have lumped God into "He's good when He is working for me and things in my life are going well" or "He isn't good because the things I want to happen aren't happening." Our anger and jealousy get out of control when others get blessed with the prayers we prayed. "He's not good" are the words that come out of our mouths. Or we say, "He must not love me like He loves them." This can lead us to spiral out of control with our views about the truth of who He is. When a prayer goes unanswered or something happens in our life that God didn't step in to stop, it's like it takes a withdrawal out of our faith jar until one day there is nothing left to withdraw. Giving up and living according to the flesh seems like a much better plan—an easier plan. It comes with results that we can see instantly but joy that is fleeting.

I also don't want us to be naïve to other part of who God is. He is a loving Father, yes. But, He is also a Father who hates sin and doesn't tolerate wrong, liars, and so on.

*We are dead in our sin.*
(Ephesians 2:1)

We are each born with an evil, and Genesis 8:21 reveals this: *"The Lord smelled the pleasing aroma and said in His heart: 'Never again will I curse the ground because of humans, even though every inclination of the human heart is evil from childhood.'"* To bring this full circle, there is nothing we can do to save ourselves or change our status before God. David Pratt writes in his book *Radical,* "No one who is morally evil can choose good, no man who is a slave can set himself free, no woman who is blind can give herself sight, no one who is an object of wrath can appease that wrath, and no person who is dead can cause himself to come to life." Nothing in our own strength changes things. David continues:

> In the Gospel God reveals the depth of our need for him. He shows us that there is absolutely nothing we can do to come to him. We can't manufacture salvation. We can't program it. We can't produce it. We can't even initiate it. God has to open our eyes, set us free, overcome our evil, and appease His wrath. He has to come to us. Now we are getting to the beauty of the gospel.

If you find yourself climbing through the ranks of your spiritual ladder in order to find God, what if I told you He is already there?

*Not everyone who says to me, "Lord, Lord," will enter the kingdom of heaven, but only the one who does the will of my Father who is in heaven. Many will say to me on that day, "Lord, Lord, did we not prophesy in your name and in your name drive out demons and in your name perform many miracles?" Then I will tell*

*them plainly, "I never knew you. Away from me, you evildoers!"*
(Matthew 7:21–23)

What if this has nothing to do with finding our way to Him but the fact that He is coming to us? Most of our lives are spent trying to make our circumstances or past mistakes better. Trying to make it right by God that we completely miss who He is and what He is doing in our lives. "I'm too far gone so I must spend time making up for it" is something I hear too much. No. No, you don't spend your time trying to make it up for it out of your own will and your own strength.

*These people honor me with their lips, but their hearts are far from me.*
(Matthew 15:8)

That's what causes us to dive deeper into sin and further away from the truth. Going to church doesn't save us. Accepting Jesus, deciding that one time, doesn't save us. It's choosing every day to choose Him. Saying a prayer doesn't give us a free pass to live however we want while we are on this earth. Now, I don't want you to think you have to earn your way to salvation, either. Ephesians 2:8–9 reminds us of that *"God saved you by His grace when you believed. And you can't take credit for this; it is a gift from God. Salvation is not a reward for the good things we have done, so none of us can boast about it."*

Friend, this is why we do the deep work. This is why we spend time working through and getting rid of the things that distract us and take us away from Him. Jesus doesn't need our acceptance. We need Him. Utter dependence on Him.

*Where do you think all these appalling wars and quarrels come from? Do you think they just happen? Think again.* **They come about because you want your own way, and fight for it deep inside yourselves.** *You lust for what you don't have and are willing to kill to get it. You want what isn't yours and will risk violence to get your hands on it.*

*You wouldn't think of just asking God for it, would you? And why not? Because you know you'd be asking for what you have no right to. You're spoiled children, each wanting your own way.*

*You're cheating on God. If all you want is your own way, flirting with the world every chance you get, you end up enemies of God and his way. And do you suppose God doesn't care? The proverb has it that "he's a fiercely jealous lover." And what he gives in love is far better than anything else you'll find. It's common knowledge that "God goes against the willful proud; God gives grace to the willing humble."*

*So let God work his will in you. Yell a loud no* to the Devil and watch him scamper. Say a quiet *yes* to God and he'll be there in no time. Quit dabbling in sin. **Purify your inner life. Quit playing the field. Hit bottom, and cry your eyes out.** The fun and games are over. Get serious, really serious. **Get down on your knees before the Master; it's the only way you'll get on your feet.**

*Don't bad-mouth each other, friends. It's God's Word, his Message, his Royal Rule, that takes a beating in that kind of talk. You're supposed to be honoring the Message, not writing graffiti all over it. God is in charge of deciding human destiny. Who do you think you are to meddle in the destiny of others?*
(James 4:1–12)

This was James's encouragement to others to keep growing in their Christian faith. It was his encouragement to not just talk the walk, but to walk the walk; to live out the word with boldness but to also recognize that it starts with ourselves first. In Chapter 4 we see James remind us that the reason why we act a certain way or sin is because of the works going on within us; the quarrels we fight deep inside that no one may know anything about. He tells us to mourn, to cry, and to hit bottom. When we hit bottom before Him we then know He is the *only* one who can help us stand and stay standing.

This isn't for those who want quick and easy. This is for those who want everlasting life here on earth. Those that want to walk lighter and free. I know you do, because you wouldn't be reading this if you didn't. The hard work is the real work. The hard work is God's way of doing things. The easy work is the world's way of doing things. Choose Him today because He chooses you!

## Does He Love Me Even Though...?

The other day, I had a full day of errands. My last stop of the day was the post office. The street the post office is on is surrounded by one-way streets and a lot of different buildings that people are frequently visiting. It is a rather busy street and a high-traffic post office. There is usually a five-minute wait or so whenever I go there. I pulled up next to the curb, put my change in the meter, and walked inside. When it was finally my turn, as soon as I walked up to be helped, a woman came in and asked if anyone parked (and she pointed) on "this side of the building." I nervously said, "I did." Then she asked me what kind of car I drive. My mind went blank. All I could muster up was that it was gray. "Well, someone just hit your car and took off," she said. I looked back at the people behind me and kindly asked them to let the woman who was helping me at the counter know that I would be back to complete my transaction.

I was nervous to see my car and what the damage was. This woman was so kind to not only come get me but to also express her concern for me and my car. "I just didn't want you to come outside and not know what happened," she said. She continued with, "The lady took off. I know where she went, and I am going to go see if I can get her license plate number for you." Speechless, again, I said, "Thank you so much."

As I walked around the corner to where my car was, I saw an older man on the phone with the police and another woman who stayed because she also witnessed it. I got to my car, looked at the side that was hit, and noticed some paint from the other woman's car and some scratches along the tire rim. That was it. If you look from the other side of the road you could probably see the paint (a little bit), but nothing was indented, missing, broken, or flat. It was honestly nothing that a little cleaning and a slight buffing wouldn't take care of. It was really that small and barely noticeable. If I am being honest, it wasn't something that I would have called the police for or wanted to file a complaint for, either. I'm not exaggerating when I say the damage was that insignificant and small.

But everything was already set into motion. This man and two women were determined to set things right and for me to find this woman and get her information. A few minutes later, a woman walked up and started apologizing. I walked with the woman, we exchanged info, I took some pictures, and I headed back to my car, where the older man was waiting for me to make sure things were taken care of. He was also waiting for the police. Everything got taken care of and everyone went on their way. I was left with my car that was barely touched but a full, overwhelmed heart that felt cared for and loved.

Whatever we deem to be small and insignificant to us, matters to God in big ways.

I don't know if they knew Jesus or not, but Jesus showed up through them. This is what He does for us. He loves us so much to take care of the small details in our life and the big ones that seem so out of control. Those people went out of their way and took time out of their day to make sure I got the help that I needed without asking. He knows you. He sees you. Let's open our eyes to our daily lives and look around. Stop looking down at your phone everywhere you walk and everywhere you go. Stop being so "busy" that you can't even witness what God is doing (or trying to do) in your life. Our problem isn't that He isn't with us. The problem is that we are just too busy for Him.

Too much of our time has been spent on trying to perform for God because we feel like that will please Him, when really He just wants to love on us as we love on Him. We have talked about how we think we need to do something in order to make up for our past.

*When God made you in His image, He rested the next day. He looked at all that He had created and said that it was very good.* (see Genesis 1:27–31)

It was on the sixth day that you were made in His likeness. Genesis 2:2–3 says:

*And on the seventh day God ended His work which He had done, and He rested on the seventh day from all His work which He had done. Then God blessed the seventh day and sanctified it, because in it He rested from all His work which God had created and made.*

This is where I would like to believe that on that first day you were created, He rested from His work to spend time with you. He said, "I have nothing else to do. I cleared my schedule for you." This is where I envision Him making and serving breakfast in bed and opening the curtains so the sun could shine through on a beautiful, sunny day. He sat down next to you to remind you how important you are to Him and that nothing else had His attention but you. He asked you questions like "What would you like to do today?" Not because He had to, but because He wanted to. This is His heart. This is the heart of a Father who says, "I know what you have done. Come to me. Come with me. Walk alongside me."

Don't forget what Matthew 3:16–17 says:

*Jesus was baptized and heaven opened, and a voice from heaven said, "This is my Son, whom I love; with Him I am well pleased."*

His ministry had not yet begun, but the Father was already pleased with His Son. He is pleased with you friend even with the ugliness inside our hearts. But, our relationships with Him can only be as close as we allow it to be. It's not He who has left. It's we who have abandoned Him. Repent. Ask for forgiveness. Say you are sorry. Not because it's "the right thing to do," but because it makes way for His love to get in.

## *Closing Thoughts:*
## The End of a Season

≡

My hands are in the air in full surrender. Although my flesh likes to try to take them down, and while the enemy says I look stupid, I am determined to have my hands in the air and open in a posture of surrender and welcoming. With a beginning of a season, comes an end to a season. The middle of the season is up to us to decide on. Will it take you 40 days or 40 years? Will it take you asking God what to do next or God saying you know what to do now do it?

*Then the Lord said to Moses, "Why are you crying out to me? Tell the Israelites to move on. Raise your staff and stretch out your hand over the sea and divide the water so that the Israelites can go through the sea on dry ground."*
(Exodus 14:15–16)

I have spent so much of my life worrying, talking, and obsessing about the same things repeatedly, but in a new season in which they may look slightly different. My hope and prayer for you after reading this book are that you go back through it and apply it to your life. We have bargained our birthright away many times for something that is quick, instant, and fleeting because in the moment it would taste so good or feel so good. Think about, for example, Esau giving away his birthright for a bowl of stew (see Genesis 25:19–34). Do you fully understand the weight, the purpose, the intention, the love that goes behind your birthright? If so, you surely wouldn't settle to trade it for a bowl of stew (metaphorically speaking) because in the moment you were so hungry for something to satisfy you and you didn't care about the cost.

> *What are you ready to lay down at His feet?*
> *What do you keep giving up your birthright for?*
> *What old wineskin do you keep trying to patch up with new wineskin?*
> *What do you allow to keep stealing your peace?*

These are all tough but necessary questions to ask yourself in order to move forward. Friend, my prayer is that you are about to end this vicious cycle of control and obsession and enter a season of rest and restoration. Ask the Lord to show you His ways and His truth in a new light and a new perspective. It's time to no longer blame your mom, your sister, your dad, your co-workers, or your friends for the way you are. You are a woman who can now say, "I am a daughter of a King, and I have a choice to let Him define me and not everyone and everything else around me."

Stand. Rise. Open your arms with me and surrender it all. When the enemy tries to remind you what you laid down, keep giving it back over to God. It's not all going to disappear when you surrender it. You are confessing that you will no longer try to control it. You are confessing that you will no longer be a victim of your circumstance. You are saying that all of you belongs to all of Him.

You are not alone. You will never be alone. Just remember that, when you begin to feel as though life is getting tough and there are things you don't understand, you don't have to understand them, and you can stand in victory knowing who you are, Whose you are, and just how much you are worth. Own that!

# About the Author

≡

Jessica Vaughn's passion to help others become confident and fearless comes directly from her relationship with Jesus. She inspires and encourages thousands by sharing her own personal struggles, victories, and journey through life. Though she's much too humble to tell you herself, Jessica is a successful online entrepreneur, founder of the Own Your Worth Member Community, and author of two best-selling books, *Know Your Worth* and *A Worthy Wife*. Her passions are being a wife to her husband, Jon, being a momma to their three cats, and spending her free time outside whenever she can (playing golf, hiking, reading, or writing in her journal). Jessica has a heart that runs hard after Jesus and credits everything she has done to her Savior.

Follow Jessica on Instagram: @jessvaughn22
Follow jessica on Facebook Facebook.com/jessvaughn22

**Want to join the Own Your Worth Community?**
It's an online member community teaching women to stop searching for their value in the mirror + men and discover their true worth in Christ. Through classes, monthly member challenges, workouts and more, this community gives you all the tools you need to find your true identity in God!
OwnYourWorthCommunity.com/Join-Now

**Other books by Jessica:**

*Know Your Worth*

If you've ever felt like you weren't good enough, smart enough, pretty enough, thin enough, strong enough, worthy enough, or doing enough, this book is for you!

*A Worthy Wife*

I believe it's time for women to begin rise up. Not with an entitled chip on our shoulders, but with strength, humility, courage, perseverance, and bold faith to be the women God has called us to be.

Learn more at fitcoachjessica.com/books

## Wonderfully Made Journals

These five journals are designed so that you can write whatever you want, whenever you want. There is no start date or end date for any of them. There is no need to feel like you are behind in writing or that you need to be consistent every day.

Learn more at fitcoachjessica.com/journals

## Devotionals:

*Wonderfully Made: Morning Prayers to Strengthen Your Faith*

Give yourself 10 minutes in the morning to read the prayer, study the scripture, and write down what the Lord brings upon your heart. My friend, there is no right or wrong way to enter His presence.

Learn more at fitcoachjessica.com/devotionals

Made in the USA
Middletown, DE
02 June 2018